Lest We Forget

Band Stands of Maine
An Illustrated History

by *Barbara Merrill Fox*

Memorial Day, c. 1900, Riverside Cemetery, Yarmouth, Maine. A somber, martial gathering (likely, of the GAR) pose beside the memorial structure as they remember fallen comrades. (Photo courtesy Yarmouth Historical Society)

Cover photo: "The new band stand on the mall at Milo Junction taken on the night of its dedication:" July 22, 1908.
Photo, right: Lubec's soldier's monument and band stand.

Copyright © 2003 Foxrun Associates. All rights reserved. Published by Foxrun Associates, Bar Harbor, Maine. ISBN 0-9741671-0-X
Unless otherwise noted, all images in this publication are from the author's private collection. All recent photos, unless otherwise noted, courtesy Richard R. Fox.
Designed and edited by Katie Murphy/Univoice Graphics, Portland, Maine

◁ They also served who, in 1861, picked up their music and marched off to war. As weapons glinted, the inspiring sound of beating drums, fifes, and over-the-shoulder horns encouraged the troops marching in formation behind the band. From their service in the Civil War, these fine musicians carried home the marching beat of the music to their home- towns. "The Washington Post March" and others like it emulated a military beat and replaced the waltz with the dance craze, the two-step. It was music that demanded a platform to perform on: a place for summer concerts, for proud uniformed bands immaculately dressed, the envy of the audience. A platform where gleeful children ran round in circles as feet tapped and hearts swelled – **a band stand**. ▷

Eastport: Sometime after the disastrous fire of 1886, this band stand was gifted to the town by an anonymous donor. This postcard, mailed in 1923 is believed to show Senator R. Owen Brewster who later became governor of Maine. There is a glimpse, at the right, of the two story building on Dana Street that housed Eastport's popular Bowlodrome, operated by "Turk" Ward.

Contents

Introduction vii

Beginnings: A Pole and a Platform 1

The "Bands" in Band Stands: Music 11

And the Band Played On: The Band Stand Era 29

A Part of the Landscape: Where to Put the Band Stand 49

Visitors Welcome: Tourism and Band Stands 69

Band Stands' Last Hurrah: Driving to Band Stands "In My Merry Oldsmobile" 85

Band Stands Tell Their Stories: A Selection of Maine Band Stands 89

Band Stands: In Revival 139

Band Stands: Gone, But Not Forgotten: A Checklist 145

References 155

Index 161

The Limerick band stand, c. 1882, today retains all the charm and nostalgia of this undated early photograph.

Introduction

In 1971, while working for AAA, I took it upon myself to plan a trek for our members that would be reminiscent of the early days when auto travel was not so easy: days when roads were dirt, road signs nonexistent and tube grease, bale wire, and a peen hammer were as much touring necessities as a lunch box and thermos. I organized a AAA "Mystery Tour!"

I was the "Mystery Scout"... and this was to be a scavenger hunt! Families were challenged to decipher clues that would lead them on a trek. While scouting the appropriate back roads for Mystery Tour stops, I kept my camera loaded with 110 film and consequently took a never-to-be-forgotten picture of a charming band stand on the village square in Union, Maine. Thirty years later, this one small 2"x2" picture provoked a personal odyssey—a search that had me traversing more back roads and following clues more obscure than those I had written years earlier!

1971: The photo that inspired me.

This odyssey convinced me that band stands are not only remnants of yesterday's lifestyle but that they should be sought out today, with as much enthusiam as lighthouses, covered bridges, and railroad depots. Band stands? Yes, they belong on this list. They were Maine's outward and visible sign of community togetherness after the Civil War. They evoke times of courage, community cooperation, public spirit, and patriotism. Even more unusual, they are today the only one of these historic structures that towns can, and are, trying to emulate! Band stands are the only one of these structures still affordable and still usable. They are making a true resurgence.

Thanks to the patience of my husband Richard, who carefully applied the brakes and jumped from the car with his camera every time I spotted a possible old band stand location, we have revisited the sites of over 150 of these original structures. And, thanks to the daily prodding and persistence of my son Lincoln Merrill, these historic structures are here committed to paper. Without Linc's daily calls regarding possible leads he had uncovered, the search to cover Maine's sizable territory would have proved overwhelming.

The stories that appear here—of the role that band stands played in Maine community life—are my tribute to all those who took the walk down memory lane with me. It is my show of appreciation to those towns and individuals who have invested in restoring Maine's few remaining band stands, and it is my hope that this book will serve as a spark to inspire others to come forward with their stories of life around the old band stand.

Barbara Merrill Fox
Bar Harbor, Maine • 2003

"Every tree is a liberty pole on which a thousand bright flags are waving." — *Henry David Thoreau*
This reenactment of the raising of the first liberty pole in Machias took place sometime c. 1913. Machias claims that the first naval battle of the Revolutionary War was the attack on the *Margaretta* on June 12, 1775. By local lore, the battle was the result of a threat by Captain James Moore to cut down Machias' "Liberty Pole." The earliest written reference to the liberty pole is found in the diary of Colonel John Allan, in which its existence in 1777 is simply confirmed.

Beginnings: *A Pole and a Platform*

Maine towns had bands! Brass Bands, Cornet Bands, Indian Bands, Boy's Bands, Cadet Bands, Military Bands, Pipe Bands, Quadrille Bands. Bands played music from "Yankee Doodle" to "Dixie"—and of course, Maine-made music like Army song leader Elbridge Locke's "Peter Butternut's Lament."

Bands sometimes played music so difficult that Harry Lewis, 94, recalls a frustrated Calais band member who exclaimed: "The fellow that wrote that (piece) couldn't play it himself!"

And Maine towns had band stands! Hundreds of band stands built for and by small communities reflected the pulse of community life. For years, they were the places where neighbors gathered to commemorate their times of greatest joy...or deepest sorrow.

Band stands were not exclusive to Maine. Indeed, they were as "New England" as white picket fences. Yet, despite being the social and cultural center of most small communities, band stands were so taken for granted that few photos were taken of them, and even less was written about them. They are rarely the prominent focus of old photographs. We find these delightful old structures peeking out behind a screen of park trees, on the edge of an old hotel view, or off in the distance, beyond the stores on Main Street. Even less written mention is found of band stands, though they were literally the stage upon which holidays were celebrated and local heroes proudly honored.

Modern life changed Maine and the way people socialized. There were fewer opportunities at home and far more opportunities in the city for entertainment. Movie theaters and concert halls beckoned, and the automobile made it possible to get there. Driving through the center of town, townsfolk literally passed their venerable band stands by, leaving these little structures to quietly fade away as the years passed. Band stands were rarely missed when finally moved, dismantled, or destroyed.

However, a few old band stand images remain, and, once prompted, memories of their place in a community's history can be surprisingly sharp! Therefore, before the only association this word evokes in our memory is Dick Clark's "American Bandstand," it is time to revisit the places and the time when band stands occupied the hearts and history of Maine.

Before Band Stands...Liberty Poles

In the early days of our nation, a New England town's patriotic gatherings took place around a "Liberty Pole."

Erecting a Liberty Pole was the way a community proclaimed support for the government. This custom was a patriotic holdover from the time of the American Revolution, when members of the fraternal organization Sons of Liberty would meet secretly under a Liberty Tree or by a Liberty Pole—a ship's mast planted in the ground as a symbol of popular uprising against British tyranny.

Many Maine villages are known to have had a liberty pole, but Bristol Mills is believed to be one of only three sites in the United States where an original liberty pole still exists. The pole stands proudly next to the Bristol Town Hall and across from the town's recently restored watering trough. Part of the lower section was replaced about fifty years ago, but the wooden top is original. A local, widely circulated story notes that the fish that tops the liberty pole is a copy of one designed by Bristol's Shem Drowne, who also designed the grasshopper weathervane atop Faneuil Hall in Boston. The copy was made at Westhavers' Machine Shop.

> The original timber for the pole was supplied by a tightfisted Bristol farmer. He had the old Yankee tendency to squeeze a nickel until the buffalo hollered. ... Several men of the village, including said farmer, were gathered at Blaney's store, and were discussing the possibility of erecting a liberty pole at the village square. When the farmer offered to supply the timber, no one could believe him.
>
> The storekeeper was especially doubtful and agreed to deliver a barrel of flour to a local widow if the farmer delivered the lumber. He was so sure the lumber would not be delivered that he added that he would roll the barrel down the village street and up the hill on the Rock Schoolhouse Road to the widow's front door.
>
> Imagine the villager's surprise when a few days later, the farmer arrived at C.C. Robbin's Mill with enough free timber to build a 60-foot liberty pole. The storekeeper, true to his agreement, held up his end of the wager.
>
> – http://lincoln.midcoast.com/-hgh/twnhl.html

These solid wooden poles, besides being patriotic emblems, were also a reminder of the lifeblood of Maine's early economy: the harvest and sale of timber. Maine's dense woods were the source of thousands of raw tree trunks shipped to England to be finished as ship masts for schooners and barks, the backbone of Britannia's transportation and trade system. Let the liberty pole show that Maine, not England, had the right to profit by the forest!

As time passed, banners were hoisted up these lofty poles and "liberty caps" were added—extra ornamentation made to resemble a cannonball. Flags of various designs, not always the newly popular "Star Spangled Banner," also flew at every town hall, post office, and school. The term "liberty pole" soon disappeared, replaced by "flagpole." As Maine's population increased, it made sense to preserve the convenient site of the original village liberty pole as the community's gathering place. An extra measure of elevated visibility for orators and musicians could be provided by adding a platform; often a town's upcoming centennial celebration provided the impetus for the expanded construction.

Stockholm provides an excellent example of combining poles and platforms.

Bristol Mills: The town's original liberty pole still stands proudly next to Town Hall.

Stockholm

One very early pole/platform stood in front of the Swedish Lutheran Church in Stockholm, Maine, and some old timers recall its role in long past town gatherings.

Frederick Anderson, 92, of Stockholm remembers that his father once invited a prominent candidate for governor to speak at the platform, but "not many people came." It was no wonder, since Anderson was the town's only acknowledged Democrat! Certainly more Stockholm citizens turned out for musical entertainment.

Anderson confirms that Stockholm's early structure was indeed used as a band stand. He even reluctantly admitted to having played tuba with the local band on the platform (though he claims he "really wasn't very good"). He remembers that another Anderson, "Fritz," was the local band director.

In 1901, a veneer and clothespin mill was established in Stockholm. By 1926 it had grown so large that Stockholm was known as "The Veneer City of New England." The bustling town and its thriving population required an expanded town center, and Stockholm's earlier, simpler band stand was torn down and replaced near the same location in the late 1920s or early 1930s. The new structure was practical and substantial, with an enclosure for selling homemade foods and a roof for protection from the elements.

During the Depression, the mill closed and jobs disappeared. People moved away. Changes in the road and the church's property eventually caused the band stand to be moved to the town ball field, away from its "liberty pole" roots.

Today Stockholm's population numbers around 300 and the town band stand is mostly unused. The proud, friendly townsfolk of Stockholm, however, maintain an excellent museum filled with extraordinary artifacts of the town's beginnings. It is worth a special visit to witness the pride that moves this small Maine town.

A platform for community gatherings encircled the lofty flagpole at the Swedish community of Stockholm.

Poles & Platforms: A Few Examples

Some rare, early photographs show a small raised platform near to or encircling a liberty pole, perhaps with decorative exterior rails. From these photos, only an octagon shape (easier to construct than a circle and providing more space than a square) has been identified. In written records, we find some references to the pole and platform combination. For example, in Hampden, a park was dedicated July 5, 1899 to Dorothea Lynde Dix, who gave her life to social reform for prisoners and the mentally ill.

> A hollow square was formed about the liberty pole and at the command of Gen. Smith the stars and stripes were raised by Capt. Henry Snow of Brewer. As the red, white and blue banner broke to the breeze three rousing cheers were given by the assemblage. ... The flag which was raised on the liberty pole was presented by Col. Charles A. Jones, Proprietor of the American House, Boston, and a native of Hampden. The flagstaff which is about 50 feet high was made by Daniel A. Smith of Hampden, who is 76 years of age. The pole was given by Melville Atwood and the topmost by George Swett.
>
> – Sprague's Journal of Maine History

Later photos confirm that a band stand was built on this Hampden site.

BAND STAND, Stockton Springs, Me.

Cumberland Mills, Westbrook (above): To the left is the liberty pole surrounded by a simple band stand. It preceded the 1882 Warren Block built by philanthropist and mill owner Samuel D. Warren and designed by John Calvin Stevens as a place for the Odd Fellows and Knights of Pythias to meet. Warren encouraged such institutions. (Courtesy Westbrook Historical Society, Walker Library)

In Stockton Springs (left), a platform is located alongside the flagpole on Main Street.

Changes in the local economy and a restructuring of travel routes cause a town's decentralization. A gathering area becomes less important and the band stand that stood there for years is consequently moved or taken down to make way for the road or another building. Furthermore, Maine's stressful winter weather and the upkeep on a wooden structure combine to hasten the building's deterioration.

Even larger and more well-to-do towns have struggled with the expense and maintenance necessary to preserve their historic band stands.

Bridgton

Bridgton's early town center included a liberty pole. *The History of Bridgton 1768-1968*, by Norman Libby, notes that

> At the intersection at the top of Main Hill, in July of 1863, an octagonal bandstand was erected by the citizens around a so-called Liberty Pole.

More is remembered about this site.

> The late George Lewis recalled a cistern at this spot, planked over and with a trap door, which could be lifted when water was needed for fire protection...large trees...stood there, set out in 1859 by young Fred Littlefield and (were) later cut down with much reluctance...a town pump (was also there). It was a so-called Dyke pump—a hollowed-out log to which a handle and spout were attached.

Obviously, Bridgton's center provided for the practical as well as the pleasurable!

That early structure was the first of several Bridgton band stands. A small town situated on the shores of Long Lake and Highland Lake, Bridgton was fiercely patriotic. *The History of Bridgton* notes that

> On elections days, Main Street did not lack for bunting. Music and oratory and perhaps a torchlight parade in the evening inspired enthusiam. At such times so much feeling was aroused that one almost felt destiny depended on the voting in Bridgton.

Is that a band stand in the background? This Bridgton postcard dated August 1909 is typical of the elusive search required to locate photos of these historic structures. This find was made possible by a notation on the card reading "They are getting ready to put a Soldiers Monument where the 'X' is." The band stand was still on High Street, and we know that in 1910 the band stand was, in fact, moved to Post Office Square and replaced with a Soldier's Monument.

The town's spirit required more dedication.

A new and larger bandstand was built and dedicated in 1877. It was 16 feet at the widest point and 20 feet high, and Norman Libby called it a monument to its builder, Jesse Murphy. At its dedication the band, under the leadership of A.C. Corbett, gave a concert and afterwards were feted at the nearby Bridgton House by Mial Davis, who served them a banquet. Because Rev. H. Barnard Carpenter contributed generously to this second bandstand, it was often referred to as "Carpenter's Bandstand."

The July 1877 description of the second band stand noted its "octagonal form, the top pagoda-shape…brilliantly lighted with lamps and gaily-colored Chinese Lanterns." Bridgton's Cadet Band was "generously tendered the use of the stand for three evenings of each week."

A familiar fate, however, awaited the beautiful building.

In 1910 the bandstand was moved to Post Office Square and replaced by the Civil War Monument given to the town by the Cleaves Brothers, Nathan and Henry. After World War II the bandstand was moved again, this time to the foot of Highland Lake, to make room for a memorial to the men who served in that war.

While the band stand stood at Post Office Square, it was the focus of many activities. It served political speakers and religious enthusiasts. Its surrounding green hosted community activities, including the "P.T. Bailey Great Traveling Menagerie and Caravan," and the "Stone and Murray Circus."

But music was the band stand's central focus. For seven years, starting in 1913, the first week in August brought nationally and internationally famous soloists to Bridgton for the three-day Saco Valley Music Festival, featuring choruses of up to 250 voices. Hundreds of people attended, planning their vacations around this great Bridgton event.

All of this activity evolved from Bridgton's first band stand, built around a liberty pole!

SOMETHING ABOUT OLD BRIDGTON BANDS
SKETCH NO. 2, 1896

In the early career of the band, the late Richard Gage, just for the fun of the thing, offered to bet five dollars that the band couldn't march up Main Street hill, countermarch from High Street to the Bridgton House and halt in front of the hotel, and all the while play their parts from the music slips without all of them breaking down in playing. The bet was promptly accepted by the band, and the trial made. The boys, unused as they were to playing while on the march, one by one broke down, and by the time they halted by the hotel, the only one playing was Wm. F. Perry! He kept right on; then Geo. Dillingno joined in, then another, and another till the entire band was in full blast again. Mr. Perry thus saved the wager; and Mr. Gage promptly paid over the money, remarking that the band had won by the skin of their teeth, but that the money fairly belonged to them.

— BRIDGTON SCRAPBOOK, MAINE HISTORICAL SOCIETY (NORMAN LIBBY)

From Pole to Band Stand: Houlton

In the 1870s Houlton's entire poulation could easily gather in Market Square, but the arrival of the Bangor and Aroostook Railroad in the 1890s changed all that. The town grew from 2,000 in 1870 to 6,000 in 1910.

Meanwhile, a disastrous fire that destroyed a block of buildings in the center of town in 1902 provided the impetus for a new gathering place. Land was donated by Andrew Carnegie to build the Cary Memorial Library and the adjoining Monument Park. The band stand was central to the layout, having been built even before the Civil War Memorial.

Forty-five members of the Grand Army attended the 1909 dedication, when a monument was placed "near the existing band stand." The town band no doubt performed. This musical group was composed largely of Pearces, Houltons, and Putnams. Houlton's earlier Silver Cornet Band had volunteered its services in the Civil War, serving in the conflict that produced another Putnam, one of Houltons' heroes: "Black Hawk" Putnam, Captain of Company E of the 1st Maine Cavalry:

In their famous charge in 1862 at Middleton, Virginia, the company lost 42 men and had 66 horses killed. Putnam was wounded but escaped into the mountains with a few others and wandered for nine days without food before getting away.

– *Around Houlton*, by Frank Sleeper

Houlton presents us with an interesting example of the evolution of the band stand from those first known photos at Market Square to the development of the town's urban park at Monument Square. Recently discovered photos illustrate that the pole—with its simple, surrounding platform—was the central support around which the band stand was eventually constructed.

1. 1880, Market Square, Houlton: A pole, but no platform.
2. 1895: "Black Hawk" (bottom, center) supervises a parade while astride his horse. A platform—built around a liberty pole—is visible at the upper left.

Monument Square today.

3. After the 1902 fire, a pole with a platform is the first structure at Monument Park.

4. On Memorial Day, 1909, a Civil War memorial was placed "near the existing band stand" at Monument Park and dedicated as a "tribute to the men and boys who answered the call to save the Union and to abolish slavery."

5. A later, undated photo shows that a roof had been added to the band stand; the pole remained as the supporting feature. (Photos 1-5 courtesy Maine Historical Soc.)

6. By the 1920s Monument Park had all the features in vogue: flower beds, a granite urn kept decorated with flowers, a boulder containing a tribute to soldiers of the Spanish American War, a cannon, and a completed band stand.

The surviving members of The 30th Maine Drum and Fife Corps. Of the band members assembled near the end of the war, only 14 year-old Daniel Skilling of Portland is identified (drummer at far right), but others would be 44-year-old Jacob Keane of Turner, and teens from Palmyra, Lewiston, Bethel, Lebanon, Acton, Skowhegan, and Buckfield. The regiment fought in seven battles in Louisiana and Virginia. (Photo courtesy Maine Historical Society)

The "Bands" in Band Stands: *Music*

Music is a universal language, understood by the simplest and the most educated of humans, by primitive and civilized cultures alike. And if dancing, as is often believed, was the mother of instrumental music, the credit for Maine's early musical heritage owes much to the dancing of Maine's early Native American tribes and their belief "that the Creator sang the plants, the animals, and even the stars into life and being."

Music Early On: The Young Nation

European settlers arrived in Maine in the 1600s. The early colonists were deeply religious people. Many braved fatigue, Indian attacks, and long distances to worship at cold, unheated meetinghouses, where they sang God's praises. But music was not a standard part of worship in all of the New World's meetinghouses, and there were widely diverse views on the propriety of music. One opinion held that "Christians should not sing at all but only praise God with their heart."

Even those who agreed that music could be used for the glory of God questioned who could and should sing. When and where was it proper? Should "only the leader...sing and the congregation should listen"? Some thought only men—not women—should sing. And that "others, who were not of the faith, should be allowed to do so."

Notwithstanding differences of opinion and lack of money, many congregations were able to raise enough funds to purchase a popular early songbook: *Ainsworth's Version of the Psalms*. Singing the praises of God then became easier—but at the same time, it also became a strenuous ordeal. Imagine standing for the required half hour to sing the longest of the psalms, surrounded by a faithful congregation unschooled in music and singing in severe discord!

Some Maine settlers were cultured men: landed proprietors, traders, and college educated, who brought to the new country a love of music and high standards of art. Their respect for their European cultural heritage was tempered by pride in their new land. Whether deliberate or inevitable, a new musical heritage was soon established as distinctly American tunes were melded to old English airs. Music would survive!

European settlers of humbler origin, unschooled in musical form, also arrived on these shores with a love of music intact. Music was made in the home for pleasure and to accompany the work of white settlers and slaves alike. Musical instruments, lovingly protected during the long journey across the ocean, were enjoyed at home and—as leisure time outside of church came to be valued more and more—at community gatherings and newly developing cultural events.

Prior to the Revolution, secular musical entertainment was rare and drama was unknown in Maine, but New Englanders were hungry for music. By the early 1800s, music lectures, music societies, singing schools, and concerts began to flourish, supported by the well-to-do elements of society, including a few "musical families" who were tutored at home by cultured teachers from abroad. These activities did not meet with everyone's approval, however, and in 1810, we read that Gorham Academy scholars "were prohibited from attending music or dancing schools."

At the first State Legislative Session in 1821, Maine quickly repealed the Massachusetts "Blue Laws" that had prohibited drama, and the now-unregulated combination of drama and music brought new joy to audiences. Although music was not generally considered a frivolous form of recreation, other forms of entertainment continued to be restricted and fines imposed.

If any person shall, for money, or other valuable articles, in any city, town or plantation, exhibit any images or pageantry, sleight of hand tricks, puppet show or circus or and feats of balancing, wire dancing, personal agility, sleight of dexterity or theatrical performances without a license therefor, he shall forfeit for every offence a sum no less than ten dollar or more than 100 dollars.
– John Lords' *Revised Statutes of Maine*, 1848

Before the Civil War (1861–1865), and even before Maine's Aroostook War (1839), attempts were made to organize local bands. After all, what was a small-town fellow to do for relaxation after spending twelve hours at his trade?

A proud reminder of Pembroke's musical heritage: This early bass drum can be found at the old GAR Hall (now the Masonic Hall) in Pembroke.

One of the first Maine bands is believed to have been formed in Hallowell in 1820. It was sometime later that decade that John K. H. Paine, a settler who came to Maine from Cape Cod and settled in Standish, put a fife, tenor drum, bass drum, bugle and clarinet together in a group that early critics laughingly referred to as "The Saccarap Band." But Paine had the right idea; he was part of a growing popular trend. Musical groups flourished everywhere and bands led the way. The country's first all-brass bands were quickly established and by 1835, America's "brass band era" had begun.

The Portland Band, active as early as 1843, was chosen as Maine's First Regiment Band when the Civil War broke out. Nearly every member of the band, including its director Daniel Hiram Chandler:

went to war and shared in the hardships that befall the soldiers.

The Civil War was the last major U.S. conflict in which soldiers marched into action to the sound of live music. Though the War left a legacy of sorrow and divisiveness, its contribution to our young country's musical heritage was profound. Countless composers, band leaders, and musicians cut their teeth on melodies composed and played for the troops.

Discipline, regimentation, and ritual were an important part of the young armies of both North and South. A description of a Union "Dress Parade" describes the important part that a regimental band played in the Civil War.

There shall be daily one dress parade. ... A signal will be beat or sounded half an hour before troop or retreat for the music to assemble on the regimental parade, and each company to turn out under arms on its own parade, for roll-call and inspection by its own officers. Ten minutes after that signal...the Captains will march their companies, (the band playing) to the regimental parade, where they will take positions in order of battle. ... The music will be formed in two ranks on the right of the Adjutant (who) gives the command. The troops will beat off. At this the band beats down from the right to the left of the column on slow time.

– *Memories of the Civil War*, by Pascal Pearl Gilmore

During the war, in the summer of 1862, an Act of Congress discharged all bands. Despite the heroic inspiration that musicians provided, their service became an unbearable expense to the Union treasury. The 36 to 40 bands per corps were noncombatant soldiers under salary who also needed to be fed and uniformed. This Act did not completely eliminate music, but instead required that any volunteer bands be supported by their regiment or made up of the "regular musicians": regimental buglers, drummers, etc. who were already part of the troops. The Act did not prevent several units from re-enlisting as fighting soldiers and serving until the very end.

Maine suffered tremendous losses in the War Between the States. At Petersburg, Virginia, alone on June 14, 1864, the 1st Maine Heavy Artillery lost 635 of its 900 men in seven minutes. The tremendous loss of lives had a significant post-war impact, especially in rural areas. Small towns lost a large portion of their young men, and population growth subsequently slowed. Also,

The "boys" who had fought in the Civil War had restless feet; they had seen something of the country and they wanted to see more. The pull of the big cities, the wide-open prairies, the huge forests of the Great Lakes Region, the many opportunities of the Far West, drew Maine people out of the state.

But many soldiers wanted only to return home. And after a time of resettling, there was a chance to reflect. Veterans found that their one fond memory of the war was the inspirational sound of military music, and they missed the camaraderie of playing in organized bands in camp or in formation on the field. Many carried to their hometowns the idea of incorporating a marching beat into their towns' patriotic celebrations. Establishing hometown bands ensured that these former soldiers passed on their musical proficiency to the next generation as they created a music of their own.

> The Civil War was the last major U. S. conflict in which soldiers marched into action to the sound of live music.

The Man Behind the Music

It was a great testament to the enormous appeal of "The Battle Cry of Freedom" that W.H. Barnes created a "Southern" version of the 1862 anthem by changing its words. Composer George Root's Union lyrics—"Down with the traitor, up with the star"—became the Confederate "Down with the eagle, up with the cross." At the height of its popularity, "The Battle Cry" was so popular that fourteen printing presses were engaged in printing the sheet music for it.

George F. Root was born in Sheffield, Massachusetts, in 1820. He founded a school of distinctively American music and was instrumental in no small degree in improving the standard of music in the U.S. He directed the renowned Penobscot Musical Association in Bangor, which at times was represented by musicians from over forty Maine towns and cities.

Root composed many hymns, but is especially known for his patriotic songs. His works include "Tramp, Tramp, Tramp, The Boys Are Marching" and "Just Before the Battle, Mother." His popular compositions "The Vacant Chair" and "Marching Through Georgia" were used in 1990 by Ken Burns in his 9-part documentary series "The Civil War."

Rebuilding community spirit after the war became essential to towns if "the boys" were to remain at home and on the farm. Music such as Root's "Rally 'Round the Flag" played an important unifying role. Rally they did—but this time, around home and hearth!

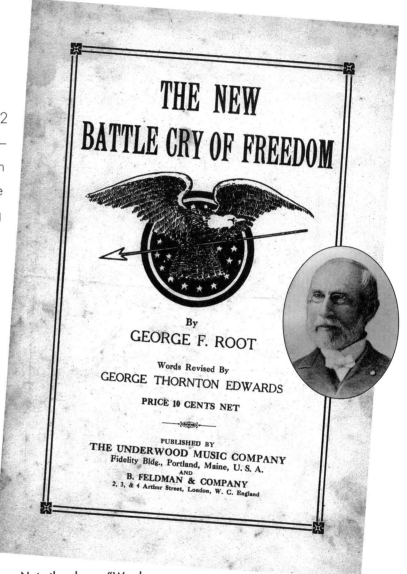

Note the phrase "Words Revised by George Thornton Edwards:" In 1918, well-known Maine composer Edwards adapted Root's lyrics to reflect a pre-WWI climate, replacing lines such as "Although they may be poor not a man shall be a slave." He changed the chorus from "The Union Forever" to "America Forever." (Sheet music from the author's collection; photo of George Root from "Our American Music" by John Howard)

The United States was still young before the turn of the century, and its cultural resources were growing, but slowly. In the 1880s, only four major symphony orchestras existed: two in New York and one each in St. Louis and Boston. Outside the cities, people heard two kinds of music: the sacred offerings of the local church and the popular offerings of occasional traveling musical groups. They learned from sheet music ordered through the mail, printed in newspapers or specialty publications (such as Hovey's *Journal of Music*, printed in Augusta), peddled by itinerant merchants, or acquired from those wealthier families fortunate enough to own a piano. The growing number of town bands now, too, became a town's link to popular music.

Themes of "home and hearth" captivated the nation, nourished by a residual patriotic fervor, as the country healed from the wounds of the divisive Civil War. Though rural Maine had limited exposure to popular music, even country folk were not too far removed from national feelings of solidarity. In 1869, Maine proudly sent 270 singers to participate in the Boston Peace Jubilee. This event was of such magnitude that a special building was constructed capable of holding 50,000, a remarkable organ installed to augment the 1,000-piece orchestra and 500-piece band, and the railroads ran special excursions. The event was so impressive it was said that

P.T. Barnum himself could not have staged the affair one bit more effectively!
– *Our American Music*, by John Tasker Howard

The band movement was gaining momentum. Veterans from Chandler's Band, who formed the Yarmouth Band, worked to recruit members. There were challenges: prospective band members often came to their first practice with little experience. Hardly any knew how to read music. It was with great patience on the part of band organizers, and much perseverance of band members, that music was made. Chandler's director, Enos Blanchard, used his past military experience to drill the boys:

Taking a blackboard, (he) taught the men the notes, writing manuscripts for them, drilling over and over on tedious exercises and holding their interest and keeping up their enthusiasm by his own love for and devotion to the art.
– *Music and Musicians of Maine*, by George Thornton Edwards

The bands learned well, and their dedication—and their popularity—lasted for years. In 1928, the Lewiston Brigade band was proud to claim the record for "long time consecutive engagements." Among the events cited by the Brigade were:

Burnside PST GAR—each Memorial Day for 37 years
Lewiston Municipal concerts—37 years
Maine State Fair—30 years, and more.

When Johnny Comes Marching Home

Maine composer Thomas Brigham Bishop composed the melody for "Johnny Fill Up the Bowl." In 1863, with the assistance of his well-known bandleader Patrick S. Gilmore (organizer of the 1869 Boston Peace Jubilee) the song became "When Johnny Comes Marching Home." Bishop may have based the tune on the Irish song "Johnny I Hardly Knew Ye," though it is not known which version came first.

Togus: Music as Medicine

In 1865 President Lincoln approved the building of "Homes for Volunteer, Disabled Soldiers." The first to be opened was the Eastern Branch at Togus, near Augusta. The chosen location was a resort bankrupted by the advent of the Civil War. Known as Togus Springs or "Beal's Folly," it was built by Horace Beals, a wealthy granite merchant who spent $250,000 to promote his property as a tourist area. It was already well known for the medicinal qualities of its springs.

As construction of the new facility began, so did the formation of the Togus Home Band (or, the National Home Band). Music would become an enjoyable activity for the residents of The National Soldiers Home. There was an emphasis on musical excellence; in fact, one of the first concert bands in Maine was established at Togus, led by bandmaster B.W. Theime, a German native and Franco-Prussian War veteran. Theime played the violin and cornet and composed waltzes, marches, light military, and orchestral music.

Even before building was complete, a Soldiers' Band had already made its first appearance, on October 4, 1867. But in a tragic turn of events, the band's instruments were destroyed by fire in January 1868. Three months later, the Augusta Cornet Band donated new instruments to the National Home Band. This esprit de corps appears to have motivated the musical group not only to continue to play, but to have built some of the earliest and finest Maine band stands.

At least four band stands highlighted the accomplished music played at Togus. By 1910, two additional band stands were added to the two already in place: The new North Band Stand and the South Band Stand. The Veteran's Home site was already well known to summer visitors, so with the completion in 1890 of a narrow gauge railroad from Randolph and the trolley line from Augusta, Togus took on a dual role. It became a popular excursion spot, sporting a zoo, hotel, theatre, and band music—at several fine band stands, of course!

A popular feature at Togus were the "trolley league" baseball games. Town teams from Augusta, Hallowell, Gardiner, and Winthrop all played each other. Admission was 25¢ and the games attracted such crowds that, after splitting the proceeds, a good baseball player could earn $5.00 a game!

This Togus band stand c.1875 (left) was built in the Stick style that came into vogue about the time the Veterans Home was built. With its overhanging eaves and diagonal boards (stickwork), this style was probably more decorative than practical. Concert-goers would have found their view of the band members restricted—and the musicians would curse the shadows on their sheet music!
(Both photos courtesy Maine Historic Preservation Commission)

Another Togus band stand (left) of an entirely different style was also built during the last half of the 19th century, c.1875 (possibly earlier, as part of "Beal's Folly"). It was a tall Italianate structure well suited to its waterfront pier location.

South and North Band Stands (above), built c. 1910. By then, the National Home Band consisted mostly of civilians. Most veterans were aging, ill, and unable to participate.

Often the men learned to play on instruments ordered from the Sears Roebuck Catalog—where, in 1899, one could buy "10 brass band instruments $100!" The brass sound dominated outdoor performances, just as strings did in symphonic concerts. The tuba added the "oomp"; the "pah" came from horns: circular helicon basses and alto horns. All played to the beat of the drum.

A characteristic of turn-of-the-century band music was the smooth, mellow sound of the "silver cornet"—really a shiny, nickel-plated version of the instrument, which was instantly popular when introduced into Maine in the 1870s. The silver cornet was such an improvement over earlier ophicleides that cornet bands sprung up in Bangor, Camden, Farmington, Machias, Monson, Saco, and Winterport. The trend died during the 1880s but regained popularity during the campaign of 1896, when the "silver-tongued orator," William Jennings Bryan, stumped from town to town demanding "Free Silver" (he believed that a change from gold to silver coinage was the key to prosperity). When this Democratic Presidential candidate came to Maine, Union's town committee hired their band for his political rally.

> **They ran a train down to meet the train from Rockland to Bath ... and we played. Lots of bands were there that day, but we had a good one!**
> – 1893 Cornet Band member Pearl C. Oakes

Appearances were essential. Just imagine the impression made by the Vinalhaven Band, seated proudly in their new band stand, sporting dark blue uniforms with gold braid and visored hats. Bangor's band turned out in red coats, white striped black pants, and bearskin hats. Bridgton's showy uniforms were blue with yellow facing, belted, and topped by plumed shakos. Yarmouth marched proudly in white linen dusters and tall hats. Is it any wonder that thousands turned out to see these colorful bands competing in music tournaments?

In a few years, women joined the band ranks, organizing their own groups and performing as all-female ensembles. By 1891, high-school-aged girls had established The Bangor Cadets, a drill team smartly suited in light blue skirts, high laced boots, and navy blue jackets and caps.

Bands enjoyed outdoing each other in the unusual and unique. In 1898, for example, Belfast's military band (organized in 1889), marched behind two unique men: "senior" drum major William H. Sanborn, who weighed in at 261 pounds—the largest man doing military duty in Maine—and Donald Orman Robbins *(right),* who, at 44 inches tall and weighing 44 pounds, could only be called the band's "junior" drum major!

Band Regalia

The decorative, military-style uniform of colorful marching bands added greatly to their mystique! Young boys dreamed of stepping smartly to the music at the head of a parade.

The Shako
A military dress hat with a short visor, high crown, and plume.

The Baldric
An ornamental belt or sash worn over the shoulder to support a sword or bugle.

The Kepi
A French military style cap with a visor and forward-sloping top

Illustration: Jayme Merrill

The Union Cornet Band is known to have played for William Jennings Bryan in 1896. Union was appropriately named for the "uncommon harmony" among its citizens. Harmony within the Cornet Band, founded in 1893, can be attributed to musicians such as (back row, left to right) Elmer Peabody, Frank Perry (leader), John White. Middle row: Harry Thorndike, Avery Pendleton, Harold Seiders, Pearl Oakes, Tyler Davis, Will Bessey, Rufus Wentworth. Front Row: Win Pease, Frank Hart, Will Morton. The young child standing the back row is Doris Messer Robbins. (Photo courtesy Union Historical Society)

The Newport Band, c. 1890: Band uniforms resembled those of the military, and parades simulated military preparedness. Newport's Dyer family were optometrists for two or more generations; it is believed that Ralph Dyer, leader of the band, was a member of that family.

Presque Isle Street Scene: On June 25, 1910, The Rockland Military Band journeyed to Presque Isle on the Bangor and Aroostook train and paraded down Main Street. Arthur R. Gould, a notable local businessman and President of the Aroostook Valley Railroad, entertained them at his Dyer Street residence, then took them for a picnic in the country on his electric trolley line! Gould would later become a Maine State Senator, serving from 1921-1922. He served as a U.S. Senator from 1926-1931.

Phillips, Maine, was the Northern terminus of the Sandy River Railroad. Entering Phillips meant crossing 74 trestles in 18 miles, one being 850' long and 40' high! This town rivaled Farmington as a destination for tourists because of its closer proximity to the mountains and the great fishing at nearby Rangeley Lake.

The Changing Face of Maine...and Music

The mid to late 19th century saw the advent of the Machine Age. In Maine, this meant the rise of an enormous pulp and paper industry and the establishment of scores of textile mills, part of a huge New England industry. By 1870, there were 93 woolen mills in the state employing 5,000 workers. By 1886, cotton plants in Maine employed an additional 10,000 workers, including thousands of newly arrived immigrants to the U.S. soil.

Bands of this time were formed both for both pleasure and for work. Every company had its outings, and the outings needed music! Factories sponsored bands much the same as today's high schools and colleges support football teams. Bands were good for morale. Music was a binding force that crossed ethnic and cultural lines and brought everyone together. Competition among rival bands drew tremendous crowds. While factory owners thought these gatherings might distract immigrants from disruptive behavior, the idea occasionally misfired and band competitions sometimes became a contact sport!

Maine's pulp and paper companies were quick to organize industrial bands who rehearsed on company time. At Livermore Falls, a squadron of musicians was proudly known as the "Tri-Mill Chapter Band of the Employers Mutual Benefit Association of the International Paper Company"! In Millinocket in 1903, The Great Northern Paper Company found a room at their mill where the company band could rehearse on Sunday mornings, but twenty more years passed before they built the grand band stand in that town.

Textile mills that developed along the Mousam River were responsible for employing over 1,000 people in the Sanford and Springvale area. One of them, the Sanford Mills, sponsored The Sanford Mills Band, organized around 1919. The band performed summer concerts in local parks and continued to so do long after its name was changed to the Sanford-Goodall Band. Sanford had a popular musical scene and was known for its early band stand and many recreation areas. Goodall Park, built in 1915 by the Goodall Brothers, Sanford Mills, and Goodall Worsted Company, boasted the "best semi-professional ballpark in the state."

Sanford's Gowen Park was the site of a handsome fieldstone band stand, still in existence. The band stand was built in 1937 in memory of Edward Gowen, a prominent Sanford bachelor, who died tragically in 1924 after his wagon was struck by a trolley car. His will provided for the building of the band stand, which was constructed on a site close to Mr. Gowen's family homestead.

Sanford: A tragic accident led to the building of this large, unusual stone band stand in 1937.

Springvale: Mill workers from the Springvale Cotton Mill would have been part of this summer scene showing the parade forming on Bridge Street, c.1898. An early, self-propelled open trolley can be seen at the left. This unusual band stand, just to the left of the Butler Block (Restaurant), was gone before the fire of 1905. (Photo courtesy Harland Eastman and Springvale Historical Society. Originally printed in *Sanford and Springvale, Maine in the Days of Fred Philpot*, by Harland H. Eastman)

At Dexter, it was not a mill but the Fay and Scott Machine Shop that supported a band organized in 1916, comprised mainly of shop employees. This band was notable not only for the support it received from the industry, but because it was led for four years by a woman, Mrs. Lillian Lucinda Snell.

The industrial age brought thousands of immigrants to Maine to work in factories and mills. These new arrivals in turn brought along the customs of their homelands, including a rich musical heritage. Immigrants were not always welcomed with open arms. But, at least when natives and newcomers together picked up their musical instruments, common ground was found. Bands were a democratic meeting ground for old and young, rich and poor, and workers of every ethnic group. This, after all, was American music!

Hurricane Island, off Vinalhaven, was a wonderful example of an early "ethnic mix." The island was a quarrying town in the 1880s.

> When the week's work was done, the energy for entertainment of all kinds sprang up out of nowhere. The Italians put together a band of mandolins, guitars and concertinas and they would don native costumes and march around the island every Saturday evening with a troupe of children following them pied-piper style. The Italian band left a lasting impression on the Yankees of Hurricane and surrounding islands. The Italian music left them "up in the air," as one woman described it, while the Yankee tunes "ended at the end."
>
> The Italians' music inspired the Yankees to form a band of their own. The two bands would form ranks at opposite ends of the island and march all over it, preserving the smoothness of melodic line despite the roughness underfoot. A bandstand was built and the bands joined forces to compete all over Knox County.

– *Hurricane Island, The Town That Disappeared*, by Eleanor Motley Richardson

Ethnic musicmakers seemed exotic to native New Englanders, and their musical participation was often commented upon. In recalling his attendance at the gigantic 1869 Peace Jubilee in Boston, John Edwards Godfrey of Bangor revealed that "the English, French, German and Irish bands were all very fine. The Irish not so good as the French."

At Island Park in Winthrop, Maine,

> ... prejudice stopped at the bridge. Former workers and laborers remembered the scene: "There was this colored fella. He was in a band ... and a dancer? Oh, my! All the girls wanted to dance with him. You forgot all about his color." "The French boys were always so neat. You know, the

The New Land

"A person has only to stand in the vicinity of ... any city in Maine where there are large textile factories, and watch the thousands of men, women and children who come pouring out of the mill doors when the bells ring at noon or at night ... the great majority, either themselves or their ancestors, from various parts of the world. Many are conversing in foreign languages for there are French-Canadians, Swedes, Poles, Greeks, Armenians, Syrians and Portugese in the crowd ...

– Androscoggin Historical Society

A Unique Fraternal Band

Fraternal organizations, formed to provide financial education and security to families, also formed bands.

From old newspaper clippings, we know of an unusual fraternal band formed in Bridgton in 1905:

A unique musical organization is the Modern Woodmen Band of Bridgton. ... it is the only military or brass band in New England composed of members of the Order of Modern Woodmen of America ... possibly the only one of the kind in America ... The leader, Frank I. Cash at one time ... was a member of the noted and high class government band at the Soldiers Home at Togus ... At tournaments at Maranacook ... he won great fame as the "boy cornetist."

Today, Modern Woodmen of America is one of the nation's largest fraternal life insurance societies.

French were the most consistent to go to the park" ... prejudice against (them), although strong off island, was submerged when the band began playing.

— "Island Park Remembered" (Stan Eames, Kennebec Journal, Historical Series II of IV, July 3, 1976)

The "Little City of Westbrook" was no small item when it came to bands. It boasted a large city band with a statewide reputation, a separate boy's band, the state's only Danish church band, and a Scotch band of drummers and bagpipers.

— *Music and Musicians of Maine* by George Thornton Edwards

In Lewiston, the Montcalm Band was made up of French-speaking musicians, and there was an Irish Band made up of their Sister City representatives.

This all-brass Lewiston boys' band, drawn from the city's large French Canadian community, was named for Saint Cecilia, the patron saint of music, who is often pictured playing the organ.

Canadian bands, representing border towns just over the bridge from Maine, came to play on the Fourth of July in parades and at band concerts. Eastport shared great festivities with Deer Island and Campobello Island, New Brunswick. Flags of both the United States and Canada proudly adorned Eastport's band stand, and the Calais Band especially welcomed the chance to go there to play with that town's well-known Indian Band.

Indian bands numbered among the earliest and best Maine bands. By 1873, parochial schools in Portland and state schools at the Indian Reservations at Old Town, Pleasant Point (Eastport), and Dana's Point (Calais) were placed under the care of the Sisters of Mercy. The talent of these school-aged Native Americans was recognized.

The young men and women of the Passamaquoddy tribe have inherited their musical instincts from their aboriginal forebears. Many of the young Native American women, trained by the Sisters of Mercy at the St. Anne's Convent School, became proficient on the piano, violin, cornet, and other instruments, while from the young men of the village was organized a small band.

Joseph Nicholas, now 85, of Pleasant Point, recalls the "small band" where his younger brother Calvin Austin Nicholas played. (The "Calvin Austin" was a steamship that plied the waters between Eastport and Boston. Joe's brother was named appropriately, since Calvin was born on that steamship!) Joe Nicholas recalls other members of the band: his father-in-law Sabattis Mitchell, Joe W. Dana, Simon Dana, Newell Noel, Steve Newell, John Newell, Soctomer Sabattis, Simon Soctomer, and Pete Stanley. "They practiced at home," remembers Joe Nicholas. "A lot of Indians didn't read but they were good musicians who played for weddings and funerals."

A special invitation came after the band had been active for several years. In 1925,

The Passamaquoddy Band played its first important engagement when it participated at the St. Anne's Catholic Church at Midnight Mass when the congregation, a choir of trained voices, altar boys and musicians was made up of Indians, all of whom were of this ancient tribe.

– *Music and Musicians of Maine*, by George Thornton Edwards

Four Native American men and three women in full ceremonial garb pose before a large crowd of onlookers at what is believed to be the Tercentenary Celebration of Plymouth, Massachusetts. The Old Town Indian nation is known to have sent representatives via birchbark canoe for the festivities, which took place June 6–23, 1921.

The "band stand" in the background is draped in patriotic banners and musicians played on the platform, which was probably used primarily for selling baskets. (Photo courtesy Michael S. Graham)

"A town without its brass band is as much in need of sympathy as a church without a choir. The spirit of a place is recognized in its band."
— *W. H. Dana, 1878*

The Turner band stand had glass windows and resembled a French gatekeeper's building. Today it has another life: see page 135. (Photo courtesy Rufus Prince)

And the Band Played On: *The Band Stand Era*

Maine's overwhelming enthusiasm for music easily provided the impetus for a blossoming of band stands throughout the state around a century ago. It was in these years, between the end of the Civil War (1865) and the official declaration of "Armistice Day" (1938), that well over 150 band stands were built throughout the state of Maine.

In the last part of the 1800s, the country as a whole was expanding: thanks to immigration and to the economic boom that followed the end of the Civil War, population was increasing. Demand for farm products and lumber was up, and industrialization was bringing a new prosperity to Maine. Natives and tourists alike had more income to spend on leisure activities. What could be finer entertainment than band music, free to all and performed out in the fine Maine open air?

And what better place for musicians and visiting entertainers to show off their talents than on a raised platform at the very heart of the town center...what better place than a band stand?

A band stand! On a warm summer night, after a day's hard work, families could relax among friends, young folks could court, and groups could picnic together around the band stand. Factory girls could show off their new dresses, tourists could bask in the delight of a vacation, and farmers come to town could wonder at the smartly attired brass band playing march music.

Of course, it's the people who make up a community; band stands simply make the "getting together" easier. But that easygoing "getting together" is only the final result of scores of fine details that came together to make a town's band stand possible, and what makes these little buildings worth a second look.

At the Community's Center

Despite being the social and cultural center of most Maine communities, band stands were so taken for granted that few pictures, and even less written mention is found of them. Books about Maine music and bands seldom mention the financing and construction of the decorative platforms on which these musicians performed. You can read town notices so detailed as to mention the repair of a barn roof or the death of a cow and still see nothing about the building of the town band stand.

Maine band stands were not the whimsical, decorative follies found in some New England towns; they instead were proud structures of both a practical and purposeful nature, used for important town events, decorated with bunting for the 4th of July, and especially appreciated by the town's musical populace. Noted Cherryfield musician Charlie Wakefield recalled a sense of relief when the town finally built its band stand: "After sitting around on steps and on planks teetering on nail kegs, it was quite nice to occupy our own band stand."

Town band members knew that if the band couldn't build one themselves, sooner or later they could count on one of the town's patriotic organizations to come to their aid. If there was a band, a band stand wasn't far behind!

The International Band Stand

Poland: An "estrada" on the grounds of Jasna Gora Monastary in Poland, the home of the famous Black Madonna shrine.

Mexico: A "kiosco" on the Yucatan, Mexico.

"Band Stand" Defined

A band stand is a common structure with no common name, whose location was seldom permanent and whose evolution is still unraveling.

Webster's Dictionary notes that prior to 1860, the single word "bandstand" did not exist. Sometimes the two-word description was found – band stand – owing to a building's specific use. It was well into the 1940s before the single word was in common usage in Maine. Prior to the 1940s band stands were often referred to with names borrowed from different cultures where similar structures are found. Some band stands were called "gazebos," after those windowed, projecting turrets, often with balconies, that well-to-do owners often built onto their homes. Today this word often refers to a structure used for picnicking or to enhance a garden or back yard.

Band stands were also referred to as "summer houses": freestanding garden structures typically found on the grounds of hotels or houses of prosperous landholders anxious to imitate the European convention. "Pavilion" was a turn of the century term describing any covering or canopy, and after gazebo, was the second-most common word used to describe a band stand (in Maine, most frequently a later, larger, square structure suggestive of the day's popular dance halls).

There were also references to music stands, grandstands, or platforms. The Italian word "belvedere," a "building commanding a fine prospect," was used in other New England areas to describe band stands set in lofty, scenic locations. Though Maine did not lack such scenic vistas, this word never caught on. In one instance, *The History of Van Buren* referred to a "kiosh" built in 1928 to "give Band Concerts by the Silver Bell Band," This was a bit of poetic license, probably a misspelling of "kiosk" (usually a small newsstand, but literally any light, ornamental structure).

It is the structure's purpose, not its name, that is important. For this study the term is used in its early, two-word form, "band stand" to refer to *An open, freestanding, public structure used by a community primarily for social gatherings of an entertaining nature, especially music!*

Types of Band Stands: Roofless

There was nothing complex about a band stand. It is the simplest form of architecture—an open-sided, raised platform without plumbing or heating. Hundreds were built; but, like snowflakes, no two appear to be exactly alike. References indicate that the unroofed band stand at Searsport, for example, may have been similar to the ones at Stockton Springs and Winterport, but not enough information has been found to determine if these towns used the same builder.

Perhaps the Earliest: FOXCROFT*

Before the Civil War, even before the building of the Old Soldiers Home at Togus, a platform was built at Foxcroft Academy that remained there as a band stand for up to 40 years. This band stand predated both the Togus structure and the band stand that was built around the Liberty Pole at Bridgton in 1863.

There is little information about the Foxcroft platform. Old photos show a simple, unpainted structure on wood supports, with latticework around the sides. It was probably first used for a celebration at the Academy in 1862. Later photos show a remodeled and possibly relocated band stand. By then the top portion had been painted white, and the latticework had been changed. In 1905 the band stand has disappeared; we can assume it was moved or dismantled.

This, and other such early roofless models, were more than rough platforms thrown up for a one-day celebration. There was a sense of pride and public spirit; the platforms were carefully crafted using unique railings, friezes, and carved spindles.

The roofless model was clearly Maine's earliest band stand design and was built right up until the 1920s, long after roofed structures came into vogue. Roofless band stands have been found at Van Buren, Oxford, Brewer, East Dixfield, Locke Mills, and Wiscasset, among others.

The Foxcroft Academy Grounds was the site of an early band stand, c. 1862. Shown are the adjacent Congregational Church and Chapel. The parsonage, home to Rev. Daris L. Morehouse (who served there 1881–1890), was moved to make room for the Maine Central Railroad Station.

*Now Dover-Foxcroft

Roofless Band Stands

Many Maine villages never topped their band stands with a whimsical roof. Though it may seem unusual, these structures were not a rarity; they were found scattered all over the state. At the turn of the century, as towns prepared to celebrate their respective centennial anniversaries, a town band stand often became a timely project, and the first step of erecting a decorative roofless platform was often taken. Many—likely all —of these structures left unroofed disappeared years ago, due in large part to exposure to Maine's harsh weather.

Oxford
In years past, Saturday night concerts took place right in the middle of the intersection of Main, King, and High Streets. This was convenient to the "Corner Store" and Dr. William Haskell's home. The band stand, which was torn down and replaced with a rock memorial to the World War I veterans by T.A. Roberts Women's Relief Corps, featured a light on top and a plaque on the side. When the state improved the road, the rock was moved to the Legion Memorial lot at the corner of Main and Pleasant Streets. (Above photo courtesy Margaret Ellsworth)

Searsport (right)
This roofless style is very similar to the band stand in Stockton Springs (below); since the towns are separated by only 4 miles, one wonders if the builder was the same or if the same plans were used.

Stockton Springs (left)
The Stockton Springs band stand appears to have provided electric lighting for evening concerts. The town of Stockton changed its name to Stockton Springs in 1889 in anticipation of becoming as renowned as Poland Springs for its tasty water.

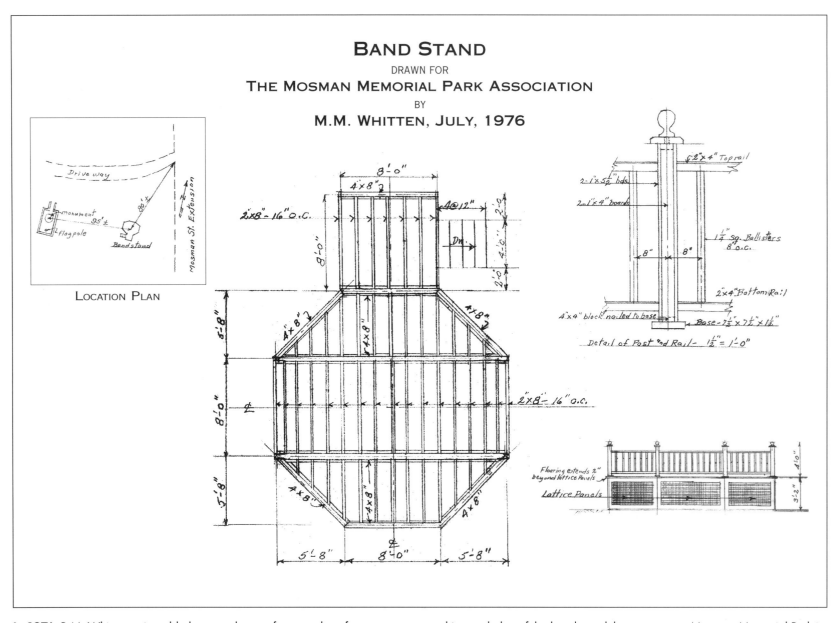

In 1976, B.M. Whitten, using old photographs as reference, drew from memory an architectural plan of the band stand that once sat at Mosman Memorial Park in Searsport. The plans were detailed and called for structural members to be of eastern spruce or Douglas fir. His daughter recalls that it was her father's hope that someday a reproduction of this fine band stand would be rebuilt. Unfortunately, it was determined that such fine workmanship would be too costly to duplicate. The plans are now with the Searsport Marine Museum.

The Traditional Model: Roofed

A roof could act as a soundboard, protect the music and musicians from the elements, and, in some towns, even provide a place for electric lighting that could be run off the new-fangled trolley wires! Of course, a roof provided decorative advantages, as it could be gaily shingled or painted. At Bath a "pinkish red" was chosen; other towns, such as North Berwick, decided on two-color roofs. Texture and shape defined the top part of some band stands and in a few cases, such as in Corinna, a roof was added to an already existing band stand.

With the exception of a few larger towns, all earlier bandstands were built without an architect—local carpenters and band members themselves simply volunteered their time to build. Consequently, simple structures were the rule. But as the years passed, some towns built band stands that were quite fancy. During the fast-developing industrial revolution, new machines were invented with the capacity to produce intricate designs in wood. Jigsaws could cut decorative detailing and complex shapes, and fancy new siding became more accessible and more affordable. Knee braces and balustrades for band stands no longer had to be laboriously cut by hand—they could be ordered from a catalog! And they could arrive at a nearby station thanks to the ever-growing network of railroads that connected far-away industries to small towns.

Corinna, before and after: A roof on a platform resembles the spacious front porch that was fast becoming a popular summer social center.
Below left: North Berwick: A two-toned roof at the Market and Main Street triangle has a two-toned roof. **Far right photo:** A genial Dixfield home.

Roofed band stands also mimicked another modern trend. New turn-of-the-century homes featured large front porches with elaborate octagonal corners. Porches and band stands alike were wonderful elevated platforms for summer socializing. Folks could relax, enjoy the cooling breezes, visit with friends, and listen to music. Both sites also became frequent spots for discussing political, religious, and patriotic topics, with plenty of fervor. Speechifying was usually common to both!

A Collection of Roofed Band Stands

Hartland, c. 1900: A typical setting for a band stand. The intersection known as Warren Square was the location of the town's white clapboarded Baptist church, and a band stand that shows the decorative detailing made possible by machine age technology.

South Paris Central (later Market) Square, c. 1884: In order to date this photo, we can consider the known facts: the obelisk monument was dedicated July 3, 1869 and the large Odd Fellows Hall was erected after 1877. The monument was moved away from Market Square to Moore Park in 1885; therefore, this photo must have been taken after 1877 and before 1885. (Photo courtesy Margaret Ellsworth)

Pembroke: A horse-drawn hay wagon rounds the corner by the band stand at Ayers Junction and West County Road in West Pembroke.

A horse and wagon pull up to the hardware store at Patten. This view of the wide, rutted dirt Main Street of Patten was likely c. 1910, when the church did not have its steeple. Patten's large band stand was lost when, during an attempt to move it, it just fell apart.

Making It Unique: Roof Styling

Since the style of a band stand is essentially defined by its roof and railings, it is useful to look a little closer at individual features. The popular architectural styles of the late 19th century styles did not go unnoticed when Maine carpenters erected band stands. A sampling of these still exist: the Gothic Revival band stand at Limerick, Vinalhaven's Queen Anne band stand, and the Victorian structures at Andover and Lewiston. Others in the Carpenter Gothic and Colonial Revival styles have been lost. Most were structurally sound—due to their builders' skill—but some completely lacked any sense of graceful proportion.

Today, less than 25 of hundreds of Maine band stands built prior to 1940 still exist. Several band stands that remain— Oakfield, Sherman Mills, and Ashland, for example—represent the vernacular two-story design appropriate to their locale.

Derby, 1904: Queen Anne

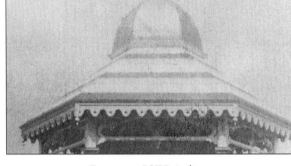
Togus, c. 1875: Italianate

Dexter, c. 1895: Carpenter Gothic

Dryden, c. 1887: Colonial Revival

Limerick, c. 1882: Gothic Revival

Lewiston, 1881: Victorian

Togus, c. 1875: Stick Style

The Finishing Touch: Railings

Newport–Camp Benson, c. 1899

Andover, c. 1890

Calais, c. 1900

Lewiston, 1881

Lubec, c. 1900

Norridgewock, c. 18?

Maine kilns produced millions of bricks during the band stand era, yet apparently only Lewiston's band stand fully utilized this product. The same could be said for the decorative cast iron added at Lewiston. Only a few—Saco, and much later, Millinocket and Yarmouth—used iron railings and those were of a very simple design.

Railings were often more decorative than protective even when the band stand stood many feet above ground level. Wood was the primary material used, and white paint was the unifying feature that would harmonize any style with the nearby church and post office. Simple uprights of alternating sizes and varying heights encircled many structures. Others were decorated with a crossed stick or lattice pattern. Ornate spindlework and whimsical designs could be ordered and delivered, thanks to the expanding railroad network.

One Size Does Not Fit All

The size of the band stand was likely determined by the size of the town band. Some villages like Athens, Jefferson, and Union had band stands that were only 11 to 13 feet at their widest point. Others, like Eastport and Millinocket were up to 24 feet across. Calais, known for its large, international band, found it necessary to add an extension to its band stand for the express purpose of housing the bass drum. Another example of this was found in Madison at Lakewood.

Some band stands had one set of stairs; others like Livermore Falls, had two. Today, some band stands feature three or four staircases along with a handicapped ramp. Strangely, many band stands originally had no exterior stairway at all; even those six feet or more above ground level were entered by ladder. In "A Native's Memories of Old Bar Harbor" published in *Down East*, Nan Cole remembers

> **When President Taft was to speak from what on such occasions was called the "grandstand" in 1910," I was bothered by how the committee would get that portly (335 lb.) President up and down the famous ladder without a mishap!"**

Other band stands were accessed through a small entry door under the platform. From here musicians climbed stairs up through a stage-level trap door, which they secured behind them to ensure a solid floor. Eastport's entry door was barely 4 feet tall. One wonders how they ever got the bass drums and the tuba through.

Maine never succumbed to the "frivolous" construction found in other states. No band stands are known to have been built on tree stumps or artificial islands, or in imitation of merry-go-rounds. The big move to replace band stands with band "shells" suitable for large ensembles also never caught on in Maine, though a few 1930s band shells were constructed. One of these platforms, made to project clearer sounds, was built in Waterville and dedicated to Maine's March King, R.B. Hall. Also built during this time period was the New

Eastport: This town's band stand rises 7 feet off the ground, providing speakers and the band a visible platform. The locked 4'6" high door likely discourages public use, and disuse. Could President Taft possibly have entered here when he visited the town on July 19, 1910?

England Music Camp's band shell in Sidney, known as the "Bowl in the Pines." At 100 feet wide, this is still believed to be among the largest outdoor music platforms in the country!

In a fashion typical of Maine conservatism, builders were slow to adopt new design and building techniques and only then if it suited their needs. The new rustic style band stands sited at scenic overlooks came into vogue at the turn of the century, and platforms were even raised to better achieve a vista of the surroundings or to allow for review of a parade. But the band stand that has Maine written all over it is the practical, two-story "I like hot dogs and ice cream with my music" style, most often found—and best preserved—in northern Maine!

Getting It Built

Q: How do you make a band stand?
A: You take away their chairs!

The joke is an old one, but the process wasn't nearly so light-hearted. Even when there was enthusiasm, there were complex matters: land to acquire, plans to decide on, and plenty of disputes. Dexter was probably typical of many Maine towns at the turn of the century when tempers flared over the site of the new band stand.

Dexter had a "town lot" or "common" used early on for shows under canvas—circuses and menageries (wild animals caged for show), as well as for 4th of July and other big celebrations. After 1886, when the school was built on the north side of the town lot, this area was not used very often.

In 1893 public-spirited citizens of the town and former residents contributed $1,000 to George A. Abbott to pay E.A. Ayer for the old "Dr. Burleigh Place." The public library building was to be built on the western side of this lot, leaving the easterly portion, between Town Hall and Main Street, as a public park. With this accomplished, the town's soldiers monument was moved from the Mount Pleasant Cemetery, a fine liberty pole was erected by the Grand Army of the Republic, and two obsolete cannon were contributed by the U.S. government at the request of Congressman Charles A Boutelle. A few years later, a band stand was built on the town's park by public subscription.

Unfortunately, it turned out that not everyone agreed with these improvement plans, and scorching comments flew whenever folks sounded off during the process. A letter signed "Old Timer" complained that

Oakfield's band stand: The more typical northern Maine model.

> Oliver Crosby's proposal looks like a gold-brick trick...It is said a sucker is born every day and O.C. has caught one and the town has got to cook and eat it."

Sarcastically, Old Timer continued:

> Oh what a delightful spot this later scheme is for a park. That beautiful sheet of water and wooded bank which nature has made. Show us one thing nature has made in this delightful spot. Did nature send down the sewage from the upper part of the village and mills? ... O, what a fragrant odor raised from this beautiful sheet of water ... If Dexter wants to have another park, dispose of the present one or build a Normal school or Insane asylum on it, we don't care which ... perhaps the last would be more useful!

In response, a letter from S.P. Crosby (Oliver's brother) describing the other lot shot back with equal fervor:

This old corner grew nothing but burdocks of the rankest kind, so thriving and impenetrable that the most venturesome boy might as well have tried to pass through the jungles of Darkest Africa. Later years there has been a cheap band stand on this lot, used occasionally when the town was so fortunate as to have a band. The band stand being a small matter that can be easily provided for elsewhere."

In the end, civic pride won, money was spent, and the parks were improved.

Dexter's Disputed Bandstand

(left) Despite the controversy, construction begins.

(below) The completed band stand on its "wooded bank." (Photos courtesy Dexter Historical Society, Grist Mill Museum)

Raising the Money

If a nearby town had a band stand, pride dictated that you build one, too! Maybe you would strive to make one bigger, better, more scenic, higher, or more decorative. Often, though, the bottom line was cost.

Band stand styles that developed in Maine towns were often fairly simple and, most importantly, affordable. In other words, the style depended mostly on what the local village carpenters could design and construct themselves. These Maine band stands were far less costly than those found in other states; elsewhere in New England, towns spent $800 to $950 for a fancy platform. In the early 1900s, Maine townfolks were more thrifty, but no less patriotic.

Pearl Oakes, an original member of the Union Band—formed in 1893—remembered how the "Band Boys" built their band stand.

> **Raised the money by playing concerts in town and out of town until we had enough to buy the lumber. Hired a carpenter, Ulysses Wincapaw, he was the only one worked on it who wasn't a band member. We built it. We paid for it.**

Examples of the cost of building a band stand have been found in several towns:

• In April 1878, plans were made to solicit funds for a band stand in Newfield. The band stand was completed the next month at a cost close to $100.

• In 1898, Bar Harbor, already a frequent destination of wealthy summer visitors, "secured just $89 for the building of their band stand." Of course, planners quickly realized that this was not enough, and it was necessary to raise an extra $40 in order to complete the job.

• Sherman Mills raised the money to build its band stand in 1903. One man on horseback was able to collect donations of $200, and a substantial band stand was built that still exists today.

Sherman Mills c. 1903: A $200 investment that still serves the community as the spot for hot dogs at Sherman Mills' Old Home Days.

Remembering the Great War

An early 1900s Decoration Day postcard.

This Lewiston monument, erected in 1868, is an 11-foot granite pedestal topped by a 6'9" bronze figure. Perhaps the first such monument erected in the United States after the Civil War, it is attributed to Franklin Simmons, a noted sculptor and Lewiston native. (From *Harper's Weekly*; courtesy Maine Historical Society)

The national Civil War veterans' organization, The Grand Army of the Republic, was formed in 1866. This powerful group of thousands of ex-Union soldiers donned their military garb for celebrations and proudly wore GAR buttons on their civilian clothes so everyone could recognize them as the loyal men who saved the Union. In Maine, the organization grew to 167 posts.

The Grand Army of the Republic was largely responsible for erecting granite monuments to honor the heroes of the Civil War. Some were simple obelisks engraved with the names of the town's local heroes. More impressive ones were square-based and topped with the likeness of a Union soldier. In Maine, the bases were usually of local granite. The stone soldier was another matter, since the cost for a custom-made likeness of a Union soldier would have been too exorbitant for many small towns. The statues were therefore purchased from national firms that cut the figures in quantity for towns both North and South (beyond the Mason-Dixon line, these statues were often financed by the United Daughters of the Confederacy). Stories are told of Maine towns that, when the statue was unveiled, were embarrassed to find their hero was a Confederate soldier!

The International Order of Red Men, another public-spirited group active in Maine in the late 1800s, actively supported bands and band stands. Their participation was important and widely recognized; an instrument-manufacturing concern, for example, was happy to note in an advertisement that the

> **I.O.R.M. Band Association of Lubec, Maine ... use and recommend the instruments made by the C.G. Conn Co., of Elkhart Indiana as the best on earth.**

The I.O.R.M. claimed its origins to be rooted in the Sons of Liberty, a Revolutionary War organization. Its colorful history also included some years as a working-class drinking society! This, of course, was prior to the Temperance movement. By World War I, the I.O.R.M. numbered half a million nationwide and at one time included former President Richard Nixon among its members.

In comparison, some towns raised funds—with the encouragement of the Grand Army of the Republic—to erect granite Civil War monuments to honor Union veterans. It was desirable for the monuments to be located in the most conspicuous spot in town, usually the town common, and the idea was partly that patriotism would assure support for the maintenance of the town commons that since the war, were falling into disarray.

But towns had to raise a considerable amount of money to afford the monuments. For example, the 32–foot monument erected by Ellsworth's newly formed GAR group in 1887 was comprised of seven pieces of granite supporting a 7–foot stone soldier. The cost? $4,000. Dexter's Civil War monument cost $2,000. The fact that it was not constructed until 1890, twenty seven years after the Civil War, reflects the financial burden the monument placed on local citizens. Wealthy individuals sometimes contributed money to build and maintain these impressive memorials, but more often the fundraising was done by local patriotic organizations like the GAR.

Band stands were more affordable than either stone statues or even the simplest of markers. The Cherryfield Soldiers' Monument was an obelisk described as "modest in height and proportion." It was 17 feet high and 5 feet square at the base. Similar to the one at Mount Hope Cemetery in Bangor, it was made of Italian marble and cost $1,200 in 1874.

During the intervening years before the money could be raised to purchase a monument, many towns built band stands to serve as the center of their celebrations. Unfortunately, sometimes when the money had finally been raised for the statue, townsfolk often took down the band stand and erected the statue at the same, prominent location. In other cases, villagers simply hooked a team of horses or oxen to the band stand and moved it to a new location. And even if the band stand was left alone, since granite is far sturdier than wood, more Union Soldier monuments than band stands have survived.

For the many Maine communities that chose to build band stands, the importance placed on the soldiers' memorial as a source of community pride was reflected by its location. More significant than the size or style of the structure was its visibility and accessibility. A place needed to be found where people naturally gathered: it should be a place to gather to hear visiting musicians and speakers, and for celebrations and ceremonies, where a band stand would serve as a focal point.

Every nook and cranny had a name; Brettun Mills, Shady Lane, The Square ... and few failed to boast of their band stand.

Newfield's band stand: What $100 bought in 1878!

Dexter's band stand. Stella Young, shown here in 1900, was an honored nurse at the local hospital. This band stand at Mount Pleasant Cemetery was a popular place for family picnics and was located near the present site of the flagpole. (Photo courtesy Dexter Historical Society)

A Part of the Landscape: *Where to Put the Band Stand*

Band stands have always served as centers for music and other kinds of entertainment, but their purpose as a spot for the community to gather meant many things. As the young country's history and sense of pride in place developed, townsfolk found that the versatile band stands suited many different uses.

A Place of Remembrance

General John A. Logan, Commander-in-Chief of the GAR declared May 30, 1868 as a day designated

> for the purpose of strewing with flowers or otherwise decorating the graves of comrades who died in defense of their country during the late rebellion and whose bodies now lie in almost every city, village and hamlet church.

Although originally and appropriately called Decoration Day, we know this holiday as Memorial Day. For these solemn occasions when the Roll of Honor was read and the graves decorated, it became convenient to have a band stand at the burying ground. In Maine, such shelters became the focus of raising the flag, playing taps, and saying prayers.

Cemeteries did not always conjure up the frightening images that modern movies or television shows leave children with today. In fact, cemeteries were often friendly places to meet relatives both present and past. Children put lilacs in canning jars and proudly went to visit ancestors they had heard about since they were very young. One hundred years ago was

> a time to know that because of our heritage, something was expected of us. These people were a standard to live by; from the time we were very young, we learned that.

– *Berkshire, The First Three Hundred Years*

Cemeteries were often scenic sites. Few vistas can compete with the view from the band stand at Mount Pleasant Cemetery in Dexter. No wonder burial grounds were often the site of family picnics and even favorite parking places for young, courting couples!

Ena Chapman of Corinth, now 96, remembers back to her school days when it was customary for the school children to make wreaths for Decoration Day and march to the Corinthian Cemetery, gathering at the "summer house" to prepare for the wreath-laying on the graves of departed soldiers.

The "Summer House" at the East Corinth Cemetery.

In Yarmouth, on the banks of the Royall River, a beautiful tract of land was purchased in 1869 and set aside as a memorial to the fallen comrades of the Civil War. It was tastefully laid out with granite-bordered lots, shrubbery, and a "garden house" with Romanesque arches and a steeply pitched roof. This tract of land was named Riverside Cemetery, and it was here that the town's marching band gathered to honor war heroes. A dedicatory monument once stood at its main gate but has long since disappeared (see page ii).

Just west of Cornish on the main road is another well-kept burial ground. The Cornish Riverside Cemetery was established around 1872. Tall granite pillars mark the entrance. There is a tomb, a building for housing tools and equipment, and a small shingled "pavilion" for visitors. The first burial that took place here was that of William H. Hatch who for many years was the oldest person to be interred there, his death coming as he "entered his hundredth year."

The use of the words "summer house," "garden house" or "pavilion" cannot discount the fact that these structures were the location of many patriotic services that included music and may also be regarded as band stands.

Band Stands on the Town Common

The band stand in Union, built in 1895, is believed to be located on the earliest "common" in Maine. First mention is made of this area in 1790; it was voted that

"Boars and rams shall not have the liberty of going on the common at large." But it was 1809 before the land was transferred to the town selectman, and that same year a new vote was recorded: on public days, "Cattle shall not be allowed to run loose but hogs shall have the liberty of going on the common at large."

In the 18th century, villages in Maine often had a common—a paddock for the temporary care of the townspeople's domestic animals. Farmers could leave cattle or other stock to be taken

Dryden: A central location, rather than a desire to beautify the town, was the reason for siting earlier band stands. The stone house in the center of this photo still stands.

Andover

The Andover band stand is a fine example of the prevailing Victorian style architecture. It is an eight-sided structure with a platform 16 feet across. Few examples with such elaborate detailing remain, and it is the balustrade, with matching frieze at the top of the eight turned posts and the almost 2-foot finial atop the tent style roof that add to its charm. Unusual, too, is that the interior ceiling is not left open to the rafters. Metal ties that hold the band stand together appear to have been in place since early in its construction. Much of this band stand appears to be original; only a few benches have been replaced.

Andover, a well-preserved example of a true common, looks today much as it did when it was first laid out. The land for the Congregational Church and the common were donated by Ezekial Merrill, Jr. in 1830. It was not until the 1890s, when Andover became a popular summer resort and stopping-off place for tourists enroute to the "Androscoggin Lakes," that the band stand was built.

Today, Andover's band stand (right) looks much as it did in the 1890s (above). Intricate wooden detailing has been carefully maintained.

Uncommon Band Stands Still on the Common!

(left) **Union's band stand in 1895**, at the turn of the century.
(above) **Union today** in the town's center.

(left) **Lubec c.1900** at the corner of Main and Pleasant Streets.
(above) **Lubec today:** In the 1990s, Lubec was gifted with a reproduction of its original band stand.

to this common pasture by a herdsman, leaving farmers free to go about the business of clearing their land and planting and harvesting crops.

In Revolutionary times, commons were also used as a training ground for the militia. After the Civil War, however, there was no more drilling and these central areas fell into disuse. Citizens considered any more sham fights to be just a waste of gunpowder. The once-busy village common became an eyesore. Arguments over its use were so frequent that many towns eventually turned over their common lands to the selectmen to manage. Local women became interested in cleaning up the area and formed Village Improvement Societies, campaigning to clean up commons and turn them into a "green." But these plots were not parks or gardens. They did not have flowers or paths. They were open green areas enclosed with hardwood trees and boasting a monument, flagpole, possibly a fountain, and ... a band stand.

Many towns have come close to losing their green area. A band stand and its surrounding park becomes less of a focus as nearby areas succumb to fast food chains, mini malls, and rural roads crowded with rushing traffic. The expense of maintaining a band stand and its gradual disuse causes towns to overlook the unique quality of a common green with an older structure as a visual focus. Even if a central open area is retained, careless zoning forces these beautiful older areas to coexist uneasily with modern convenience stores and gas stations.

The Band Stand in the Park

The city of Portland established its first real park—Franklin Park—as a firebreak after the Great Fire of 1866. This was a forerunner of the post-Civil War movement to create green spaces in Maine cities.

Maine villages were slower to adapt to the idea of scenic parks. Until the 1900s, the attitude in many villages was that it was wasteful to plant trees or flowers on the green just for ornamental purposes. But as automobiles became more popular, towns' central greens often became criss-crossed with intersecting roads. The resulting bisected green areas were often left uncared for and became

Wiscasset Common: Laid out as a training ground for the militia during the Revolutionary times, it fell into disuse after the Civil War.

The military, agricultural, and ecclesiastical uses that earlier defined a common gave way to grassy "greens" near a village's public buildings and "squares" located in urban centers—each public meeting area was a likely band stand location.

COMMON, WISCASSET, ME.

THE PARK, LIVERMORE FALLS, ME.

Livermore Falls: More leisure time, a flourishing economy, and ever-increasing traffic led to an eagerness to landscape the town's patriotic gathering places. Band stands bcame the center of planned parks. Here at the corner of Main and Union Streets was located a band stand with two staircases. The neighboring village of Livermore built its band stand near the town's post office.

Deering Oaks, Portland: Parks were established to promote the physical and mental health of city dwellers. In 1883, before either the pond fountain or the duck house was built, Portland City Civil Engineer William Goodwin commissioned a "fine" band stand to be built; it was located on the northwest corner of the park.

In May 1952, when the underpinnings had rotted away and it became unsafe, the City's Director of Parks and Recreation declared "it isn't worth restoring and there's no money right now to build a new one." A new band shell was donated by Frank Gaziano of National Distributors Inc. in 1984, but it lacks the ambiance of the original band stand. (Photo courtesy Maine Historic Preservation Commission)

A Rustic Retreat

Advances in communication and transportation changed rural Maine life considerably. There was a need for respite from the newer, faster pace of life, and people longed to "return to nature" during their leisure time. Band stands were nestled in a pine grove or on a knoll to overlook the ocean or lake and constructed of natural materials in a rough-hewn or rustic style to imitate popular mountain lodges.

Band Stand, Clifford Park, Biddeford, Me.

Sebago Lake, ME. The Grove

Lakewood, Madison, ME. 110.

Clifford Park in Biddeford (above left) was home to Painchaud's Band, thought to be the second oldest in New England. They served as the official band of the Maine National Guard in 1889. Pierre Painchaud was a "quick change artist" known to dash from the stage between numbers for costume changes. Drum major Joseph Harvey, when fully arrayed in uniform and shako hat, stood an impressive seven feet tall! At one time, a college boy invited to "sit in" with the band was the young saxophonist Rudy Vallee.

A rustic structure (above right) in an unidentified Sebago Lake location.

(left) **Lakewood Summer Theatre** opened in 1898 in a wooded grove on Lake Wesserrunsett, Madison. The show included a trolley ride from Skowhegan and cost 25¢. The band stand's extension, on the right, was for the bass drum.

Four-Sided Band Stands: a.k.a. Pavilions

Scenic areas sometimes sported square band stands. They oriented the audience toward one stage-like side, eliminating some of the sociability that was inherent in the octagon and hexagon styles so well suited to the crossroad band stands of Maine villages.

York Beach: The band stand at Short Sands closely resembles the park's trolley waiting platforms.

Four-sided band stands were appropriate for locations with a view, where crowds gathered to enjoy the scenery as well as the entertainment. These were roofed band stands, not the earlier roofless style platforms found in villages like East Dixfield. These structures were often known as "pavilions," and with this new name came an increase in size. One pavilion still in use at Crosby Park in Dexter measures 36 feet by 28 feet.

Square or rectangular band stands were located in the grove at Fairfield's Island Park and along the Kennebec River in Skowhegan. In 1932 a large four-sided band stand was built along the Penobscot River in Old Town. With more time for leisure activities, Maine citizens found many uses for these structures: they were no longer simply stands for a band to play on.

Dexter: Crosby Park

Belfast: The "pavilion" at City Pool Park.

Rockport: At Oakland Park, visitors could listen to a band, watch a ball game, and enjoy the ocean view. Dancing, skating, and dinner were accessible here, thanks to the trolley line.

unsightly dumping areas. Families with homes abutting the green complained; they wanted pleasant scenery to view. Soon there was an eagerness to landscape the green. Town band stands were eventually surrounded by trees, in a setting strewn with gardens, fountains, and sculptures. Park benches along paths became an integral part of the design. Designated areas for strolling were also meant to discourage pedestrians from walking along the side of the road and perhaps carelessly stepping out into the dangerous path of an oncoming "tin lizzie"!

Acadian Hotel, Castine: This ornate structure combines a four-sided structure suitable for enjoying the ocean view with a more traditional octagon-shaped band stand on the upper level.

Skowhegan

A four-sided band stand was located at Coburn Park in Skowhegan, not on the site of the present band stand but down the hill, closer to the beautiful Kennebec River. What is now the park was originally known as the "Russell Lot," owned by former Governor Abner S. Coburn and his brother Philander Coburn. They donated half of the land for the park in 1885, and the other half 20 years later. The property was an ideal spot for a park: a shady glen for strollers and a pond to picnic around. Skowhegan's first band stand was likely built here for the Company E Military Band, led by R. F. Washburn between 1907 and 1917. The band stand's demise is unknown, but in 1970, a second one with a concrete base was built by Lawrence Sylvain. Despite the charm of the setting, people protested that it was difficult to sit comfortably up on the side of a hill. At the hilltop, quiet parts of the music couldn't be heard, and musicians roasted in the old structure! Finally, in 2000, the Coburn Park Concert Series was given a new home in new, larger (20'), octagon-shaped gazebo (as it was called) on level ground, in the shade.

Local Skowhegan resident Maurice Valliere remembered when former Democratic Congressmen Samuel W. Gould made a speech at the square Skowhegan band stand. Valliere remembers Gould complaining about Republican Herbert Hoover's fishing trip boasts. Gould's comment ran something to the tune of

> **If he says he could catch a fish out where there hasn't been a fish in years, we are in real trouble!**

Another band stand of a more elaborate octagon style was located next to the old Skowhegan House and convenient to their railroad station.

Skowhegan's earliest: A four-sided band stand.

The Eastern Promenade, Portland, c. 1890: A John Calvin Stevens design located at Fort Allen Park.

Shingle Style

The influence of Portland architect John Calvin Stevens can be seen in shingle-style features found on several Maine band stands. Stevens developed this unique look, which was a dominant feature of homes built throughout New England during the band stand heyday of 1880-1920. Stevens designed two band stands for Portland, one on the Western Promenade and one that still stands proudly at Fort Allen Park on the Eastern Promenade.

Stevens' designs stressed the natural appearance of wood. His trademark shingles circled the band stands and appeared on posts, balustrades, and even roofs.

Noted architect E. E. Lewis used Stevens' shingle-style design ideas when he planned the First Baptist Church of Houlton, and when he designed the city of Gardiner's 1890 band stand, which appears to be very similar to Stevens' design of Portland's Western Promenade band stand.

Gardiner's Village Green band stand (upper right), designed by architect E. E. Lewis. (Photo courtesy Maine Historic Preservation Commission)

Portland's Western Promenade band stand lower right, the design of architect John Calvin Stevens.

Kingfield, May 24, 1990: The Kingfield band stand travels to its new home at One Stanley Avenue. Moving band stands is not a new idea. Maine farmers were experienced loggers and adept at moving heavy objects with the aid of oxen or, later, horses. Maine band stands rested directly on the ground with little or no foundation, so relocation was a relatively simple operation. Of course, it was made simpler, too, by the fact that the early moves did not have to contend with modern-day telephone lines or heavy traffic! (Photo courtesy Dan Davis)

Band Stands on the Move

The reward for the farm family who left off work on Saturday and bounced along the roads was the camaraderie and excitement of going to town! Folks in wagons and buggies often greeted their neighbors around a newly constructed band stand near the village crossroads. Almost always there was a church nearby, as well as a store and a post office. At the start of the 20th century, there were only about 144 miles of paved roads in the entire United States, and any more than an hour bumping along a dirt road was a hard drive. Consequently, many small Maine communities, while close together by modern standards—for example, Pembroke and West Pembroke, Oakfield and Island Falls, East Dixfield and Dryden, Skowhegan and Norridgewock, Derby and Milo—each had its own band stand.

At the crossroads, families could sit in their carriages and listen to a band concert. As automobile travel became more prevalent and the roads were widened, the band stand was often crowded onto just a small island of green in the middle of traffic. Fortunately, these structures were not set in concrete so some were eventually moved to new locations. Sometimes the moving of the band stand also marked its demise. This appears to have been the case in Round Pond and in Patten, where

they tried to move it by the old railroad station and it broke apart.

On at least a few occasions, concerned individuals took it upon themselves to have the band stands moved—sometimes to a safer location, other times so it could be converted to a garage or store! When the town arranged to have the band stand relocated, it was likely to a site more in keeping with the development of the town. Norridgewock's second band stand, for example, was moved when the Village Improvement Society erected the War Monument to honor the Civil War dead. Charles Miller is credited with this change, and the band stand sat for some time in the location now occupied by the World War II Honor Roll. In either case, these moves saved some band stands from demolition and allowed us to still enjoy them today.

Another reason to move the band stand was the arrival of the railroad in town. Space had to be found for a railroad station and fires could be a horrible result of the iron horse. Anything—buildings, hayfields and even band stands—were at the mercy of sparks thrown off by metal wheels against metal rail or burning debris from the coal and steam-fired engine.

Moving the band stand was always an event. Paris Hill's band stand was moved in 1887 and some old notes uncovered by Martin Dibner tell us

The bandstand was moved to the common Thursday and placed just back of and midway between the two elms nearest the town pump. It is a pity it could not have been loaded in such a way

Music close at hand: Summer was the time for outdoor entertainment, but it had to be accessible. Band stands were built close enough together to be easily reached by horse and carriage. (Map courtesy Barry Jackson)

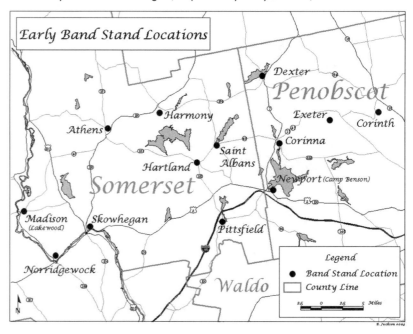

that it could have been weighed, for several persons were anxious to treat the crowd if it weighed over twelve hundred, while others were equally as anxious to stand treat if it weighed less than a ton!

Life Around the Band Stand

From the *History of St. Albans, 1799-1981*, we read about a town turn-of-the-century Independence Day celebration and the finale that rang out long and loud around the band stand.

A procession of Civil War veterans and school children led by Franklin Luce playing the flute he had used in the War. Bearing their sprays of flowers and small American flags, the boys and girls marched to the village cemetery for the playing of taps and a prayer of the Union Church minister. Many drove in from the farms to watch the parade and eat picnic lunches while visiting with friends in the village. In the afternoon all gathered at the Town Hall to salute the flag, sing "America" and listen to an address by a Maine political, legal, or religious dignitary.

The St. Albans band stand is gaily decked out for a Fourth of July celebration, or for its 1913 Centennial Celebration in this early, undated photo postcard.

On the Fourth of July the day began at midnight on the third. At that hour, the Church bell and the school bell rang for half an hour with the young men of the town taking turns at the bell ropes. Noise, shouting and general activity went on until dawn when everyone went home to get a little sleep before the day's celebrations.

Again there was a parade, this time for fun with all taking part wearing laughter-provoking costumes. At night the Hartland-St. Albans Band gave a concert in the band stand located on the hill above the post office. A spectacular display of fireworks from the same location ended the celebration in St. Albans.

St. Albans celebrated its 100th birthday on June 13, 1913.

For months preceding, the committees worked. Their efforts were rewarded by a big turnout of visitors on a perfect June day. From December 12, 1912 through April 16, 1914, the Centennial Treasurer, A. P. Bigelow, collected $656.54 to pay the expenses of the celebrations. Eighty-eight contributions were made, ranging from 50¢ to $10. This sum paid

The village of Webbs Mills at the quiet intersection of Routes 11 and 85 in Casco was likely photographed from the nearby Free Baptist Church on the hill. The country store still retains the original look of this corner.

for the music was $104.20; beans for the free dinner ran $18; and bunting and flags to decorate every building in the village cost $104.

It didn't take a holiday for bands to get up a summertime concert and create a band stand event. Concerts were delightful for families. Children especially had a good time, since some band stands doubled as lemonade and hot dogs stands, or a peanut vendor was conveniently stationed nearby. And maybe someone had turned the crank of the ice cream maker just before the start of the music!

Grown ups would lie on the grass, socializing and sharing supper. Children sat on the edge of the band stand platform, licking ice cream and dangling and kicking their feet to the music. Then, as the band stirred the crowd with tunes that invoked pride and patriotism, the younger crowd would jump down and march 'round and 'round the band stand, often to melodies made famous by John Philip Sousa and some of Maine's very own composers—"March King" Robert B. Hall, Winfred S. Ripley, or Liberty Chorus Director George T. Edwards.

There were differing degrees of musical ability. Civil War regiment band veterans may have had high standards and local band members may have had exceptional talent, but in the heyday of town bands and band stands, there were waiting lists of young men with and without musical ability who wanted to join a band.

Norridgewock: The whole town turns out for the festivities! (Photo courtesy Maine Historical Society)

It was of little matter. The music might have been a little rough around the edges, since, after all, they played for the fun of it, and the town supported them...whether they played well or not.

R.B. Hall: Maine's Famous Son

John K. Paine, born in Portland in 1839, may be credited with being the first composer of truly American classical music, but Maine's foremost "March King" was Robert B. Hall. Hall composed over 100 marches, some of high recognition. John Philip Sousa played a Hall march at the 1900 Paris Exposition.

Born into a musical family in 1858 in Bowdoinham, Hall's father taught him to play cornet. After his father's death, the young Hall found a musical mentor in Melville Andrews, founder of Andrew's Music Store in Bangor. Hall's playing range was so tremendous that "While marching in parades, he would play certain strains an octave higher than written. You always knew when his band was coming your way."

Hall dedicated many of his marches to organizations with which he was associated. "The Red Men March" was written for Bangor's I.O.R.M. Other marches were composed for fraternal organizations: "Patriarchs Militant" (for the Odd Fellows of Waterville), "Dunlap's Commandery" (for the Knights Templars of Bath), and "Exalted Ruler" (for the Waterville Lodge of Elks). His work has continued to be well respected for years; Hall's "March Funebre" was played at President John F. Kennedy's funeral in 1963.

Tragically, Hall suffered a stroke and died in poverty in 1907 at the age of 44.

The dapper R.B. Hall Band, instruments in hand, pose in 1878 on a wide, rutted Richmond dirt road. (Photo courtesy Maine Historical Society)

ON MAY 11, 1981 MAINE GOVERNOR JOSEPH BRENNAN APPROVED A BILL TO ESTABLISH **R.B. HALL DAY.** IT IS CELEBRATED EACH JUNE, WHEN COMMUNITY BANDS CONVERGE STATEWIDE TO PLAY HALL'S FAMOUS BAND MUSIC.

South Brooksville had a deep harbor with a "sticky bottom" and was a convenient stop for the Eastern Steamship Line. This very early band stand was a gathering place for tourists as well as the workers at the quarries and gristmill. It was conveniently located near the home of Ford Gray, once the South Brooksville Band director.

Visitors Welcome: *Tourism and Band Stands*

Early Maine settlements were based on lumbering, farming, and shipping. Later, when mills became the focus of some towns, homes were often within walking distance of the workplace, as was the case in harbor, lumber mill, and quarrying villages. Entertainment at the crossroads band stand was for and by local townsfolk and their immediate community. This was all about to change.

Transportation Brings Tourists: Steamships and Summer Colonies

By the 1870s, the slogan "Maine Is the Playground of the Nation" was drawing thousands of travelers to the state. The introduction of the steamboat initiated this influx of tourists, and vacationers who arrived by boat continued their journeys throughout "vacationland" by train and trolley. Steamboat companies ran advertisements in out-of-state newspapers proclaiming the beauty of Maine. In 1897, 100,000 sightseers traveled up the Kennebec River, encouraged by Kennebec Steamboat Company brochures. The Eastern Steamship Line brought passengers to Cape Rosier, near Castine, as well as to the "big dock" at South Brooksville's Herrick House. Entire families could now vacation in Maine; father joining the family at week's end by boarding a Friday night Eastern Steamer in Boston and arriving in Round Pond, Rockland, or South Brooksville the next day.

Tourists in the late 1800s often had the same desire as present-day travelers to the state: to enjoy, for a short time, the slower pace of life that had been traded for the wealth that city industrialization had brought. These visitors primarily socialized with each other at their tennis courts, yacht clubs, and dining rooms. They did, however, enjoy the "quaint" local bands who met them on the steamship wharf! These out-of-state passengers now joined local townsfolk and immigrant workers from the busy nearby granite quarries and gristmills in enjoying summer entertainment at the band stand.

Steaming into port, this ship was one of many that opened new possibilities for Maine communities, including Round Pond. Prior to steamship service, it was necessary to go by rail to Damariscotta and then via stage-line to reach Round Pond.

Railroad Passengers: Profit!

As early as 1879, Maine's popular steamship travel lines were linked to 31 railroad companies. Eventually, there was one mile of track for every 644 people! Some lines, like the 7½ mile Whitneyville and Machiasport Railroad, were used to transport freight alone; the rails delivered the goods from the mill to the nearest seaport. Other companies covered several hundred miles; scattered along the way were 188 stations and many fine residences. It didn't take long for enterprising businessmen like Maine Central Railroad's Payson Tucker to realize that adding substantial summer tourist ridership could boost railroad profits. New band stands were erected close to bustling depots: entertainment was the draw and profits the motive.

It was Tucker who coined the slogan "Maine: the Front Dooryard of Our Country" and directed publication of the first Maine guidebook for tourists in 1885.

Maine's economy in the early 1900s was to a great extent dependent upon wealthy tourists from all over the East who packed their trunks and traveled north to spend weeks, and often whole summers, at a Maine destination. The rails met the steamships and carried visitors to the scenic interior lakes and the northern woods. Small towns such as Island Falls saw their populations double between 1893 and 1900. A town without rail service was a town with little hope of growth.

One 1890 publicity stunt was created to draw passengers for longer rides advertising the play "Old Jed Prouty" to be held at the Bucksport Tavern. Maine Central Railroad "fitted up" a baggage car to resemble the office of the Bucksport Tavern, using actual tavern furniture. Along the route from Portland, Maine to Portland, Oregon, receptions were held and 500,00 brochures were distributed, urging all to "Come East, Young Man!"

Rail lines created more ways to profit from their passengers. At various times in their history, railroads such as the Maine Central not

Dryden (Wilton), top: Lumber and commercial products were a major source of railroad income and this village bustled with woolen and grist mills, shoe shops, and summer camps. The band stand is gone and the nearby railroad station has a new recreational use—as a clubhouse for snowmobilers.

Presque Isle, bottom: Here, the band stand was built near the railroad station. Many places did so in order to serenade arriving tourists!

Railroads Make Tracks: Camp Benson

Both the steamship and the railroad contributed to the development of Camp Benson at Newport. Named after a Civil War surgeon, it was a military encampment and parade ground for the GAR. When it was mapped out in 1892, plans called for a band stand to be built in the section bordered by Water and Bennett Streets. An 1899 newspaper story proudly notes that

> **The band stand at Camp Benson is approaching completion. Octagonal in form with a sort of pagoda roof, the floor is of hard pine and prettily laid and is reached from the ground by a stairway on the outside, protected by a balustrade of elegant design. Below is a room to be used for instruments, books, etc.**

Camp Benson, because of its accessibility and its dance pavilion built on a scenic peninsula overlooking Sebasticook Lake, was a wonderful spot for dances, outings, company field days, and ball games. In fact, it was so popular that as early as 1910 the GAR voted to charge admission for its encampments.

Sadly, all that remains of Camp Benson today is a small brick Cape Cod-style home that still has numbered rooms and is believed to have been the hospital.

Camp Benson: A close examination of this early "yard-long" photo at Milo Historical Society shows women as players as well as spectators.

only served, but owned and operated grand resorts—with band stands on the grounds, of course—as well as coastal steamers and ferries. Maine Central Railroad even ran bus lines, and at one time held partnership in an airline! In bygone times,

> ... colors of the Maine Central went to sea, flying from the foremasts of thirteen white, gilt and mahogany steamers and from four of the largest ferries ever operated on the coast of Maine.
> – compiled by John F. Legg

The newfound prosperity for some meant long hours of hard work for others. Rural Mainers who worked the railroads got a glimpse of life among the "rich and famous"—a lifestyle most had never seen before. Their seemingly endless supply of dollar bills encouraged some new ideas among the local populace, and one droll observer encouraged his fellow townsfolk to

> ... milk the city people instead of the cows!

By the outbreak of World War I, personal transportation was on the increase. New wealth brought more automobiles, and rail ridership decreased. The railroads were already in trouble: Maine's shipbuilding industry was on the decline, and granite quarrying was losing out to the manufacture of concrete. The grand resorts of the "gilded age" were not as profitable as they had once been.

When World War II broke out, the transporting of thousands of carloads of food for the war effort added to passenger traffic and increased business for the duration. But when hostilities ended in Europe and Asia in 1945, there was another drop in railway business. Automobiles, tires, and gasoline became readily available during the postwar boom, and railroads faltered. The decrease in passenger rail business also caused some band stands located near railway stations to be abandoned, and, along with them, town bands dwindled, then parted company.

VACATION TRAVEL
The United States Railroad Administration Removes All Restrictions

One year ago, under the pressure of war necessities, the public was requested to refrain from all unnecessary travel and under the stress of war conditions, the public was unnecessarily subjected to a great deal of inconvenience when it did have to travel.

Now the war necessity is passed and it is the settled policy of the Railroad Administration to do everything reasonably within its power to facilitate passenger travel and to make it more attractive.

In furtherance of this policy, the Railroad Administration is entering upon a moderate program of advertising, to remind the people of the extraordinary opportunities for sight-seeing and for pleasure-seeking which our country affords—the National Parks, the seashores, the lakes, the mountains, the woods and the many places of historic interest.

The vacations season is approaching, and the time is at hand to plan for the change of scene, for rest and recreation. It will be the effort of the Railroad Administration to aid in such planning and to make your travel arrangements convenient and satisfying.

The staff of the United States Railroad Administration will be glad to furnish illustrated booklets and provide necessary information as to fares, train service, etc. Such information may be obtained from the local Ticket Agency or the nearest Consolidated Ticket Office, or by addressing the Official Travel Information Bureau at 143 Liberty Street, New York; or Transportation Building, Chicago; or 602 Healy Building, Atlanta, Ga.

Every official and employee of the United States Railroad Administration is a public servant. Call on them freely.

**Director General of Railroads
Washington, D.C.**

A Maine Central Railroad advertisement encourages passengers to resume rail travel that had been interrupted by World War I. (framed notice displayed at the Burger King restaurant, Presque Isle)

The North Woods: Island Falls

At Island Falls the houses were always filled with people happy to have an evening together with games and singing, mostly the (Civil) war songs of the period. At that time, in all the town there were only two musical instruments, a violin which George Darling played principally for kitchen dances, and a piano which the Pratts, quite newcomers, brought with them.

– Nina Sawyer, *A History of Island Falls, Maine*

Island Falls did not lack for entertainment even before this band stand was built. One July week in 1903, 5,000 marched in the Orangemen's parade, Sig Sautelle's circus performed, and a vaudeville show under canvas played all week!

As early as 1878, in order to reach the rich hunting and fishing outpost of Island Falls, sportsmen came by railroad. The nearest debarkation point was at Mattawamkeag Station, and the last 36 miles to the "sportsman's paradise" entailed a trip by buckboard. Local people got to know eminent visitors: William "Bill" Sewall, the "First Child Born of Pioneer Settlers, Island Falls," for example, became Theodore Roosevelt's respected guide and a friend for life.

Rodney C. Barker's Steamboat Excursions to Norway Island in Mattawamkeag Lake were popular in the 1880s but when the Bangor and Aroostook Railroad came all the way to Island Falls on November 23, 1893, tourism, trade, and industry truly began to boom. Population grew from 223 before 1900 to 1,063 after the century's end! Six daily trains brought a fast end to the stagecoach era.

Life was changing. In June 1904, fifty-four tickets were sold at the station for the circus in Bangor and the Island Falls Mill Company shut down their plant so its employees might attend the circus.

Rich forestland and easy transport beckoned business. Northern Woodenware Company employed close to 175 people in Island Falls producing lumber, wood bowls, clothespins and more. Howard B. Smith was the company's General Manager. He and his wife were talented musicians, and Mr. Smith organized a band and built the band stand at a prominent corner at the center of town. It remained there, near the present location of Katahdin Bank, until the 1990s.

The Island Falls band stand is visible in photos of parades held here in the early 1900s. Ominously, the Second Ku Klux Klan held its first daylight parade in Island Falls in 1925. The Maine KKK of that time was concerned with the "problems" of government and labor disputes and made immigrants, Catholics, and Jews its target.

Grand Hotel, Grand Music!

The first band stands provided free music and entertainment. By the early part of the 20th century, however, hotels, resorts, and amusement parks were building band stands for their paying guests, part of a lavish spread of tennis courts and bowling alleys, indoor swings and other outlandish features.

Shortly after 1875, when the Maine Central Railroad instituted the Lake Maranacook crossing in Winthrop, the railroad built the Lake Maranacook Hotel. Winthrop had long been regarded as one of the earliest towns in Maine where people took a deep interest in music. The hotel quickly developed a resort center with plenty of entertainment. There were many facilities at the Hotel for concerts, lectures, sports, and among them was a band stand.

In the beginning, brass bands, numerous in Maine at the time, were invited to play in the Maranacook contests, which lasted for several days. Prizes went as high as $500.

In 1880 Edward Raynes was leader of the band and on July 5th of the following year, at a band tournament held at Lake Maranacook, this little band, which consisted of eighteen pieces, played its selection in such a manner that it thrilled the twenty-thousand people who had assembled and won for it the third prize.

– Music and Musicians of Maine by George Thornton Edwards

The Yarmouth Brass Band's third-prize win was for "The Rip Van Winkle Overture." William Rowe, in *Ancient North Yarmouth and Yarmouth*, explains that this was only a year after the first reed instrument, as well as the first slide trombone, was used by the band.

Train service from Portland brought 80 cars to Lake Maranacook in that year, carrying thousands to the competition! Trains were a popular mode of travel for both musicians and spectators. At times there could be 48 bands participating in a single competition and trains filled with trumpets, tubas, and tourists meant profit for the transportation industry.

The last of the great Maranacook tournaments was held in 1886, and nearly all Maine bands participated. The end of the large tournaments was not the end of music or vacationing at this location, and the hotel's business continued though. There was enough activity that when, on August 25, 1905, the legendary Lake Maranacook Hotel burned. It was rebuilt and being painted by June, 1907.

The railroads were not to be counted out. After all, they also owned many of the state's trolley lines, and they had big plans to attract the public!

MARANACOOK LODGE, MARANACOOK, MAINE

The Maranacook Lodge, Lake House and Belgrade Hotel were part of Winthrop's flourishing era of summer hotels.

Band Stands at Trolley Parks

You enter by the front and you exit to the rear;
The operator drives,
    but he doesn't have to steer.
An uptown view with time to relax,
    lookin' out the window,
    rollin' down the tracks.
20,000 people ride 'em every day,
    a fantastic ride for a small fare to pay.
Once they ran by steam, and once by mule.
Now electric power is the streetcar's fuel.

– Saint Charles Streetcar Song

Such were the words from an old song that described the popularity of New Orleans streetcars in 1835. Everywhere in the country, the experience of riding streetcars—"trolleys" or "electrics"—was the same. Trolleys took workers to and from their factory, store, or office. They were cheaper to operate than trains, had the advantage of being able to make more frequent stops, and surprisingly, they were faster! During the summer tourist season, the enclosed passenger cars could be replaced with open cars, referred to as "breezers," to assure a more refreshing ride. Whizzing along at 10 miles per hour was a cooling way to spend a summer evening, and trolley rides became a popular pastime of the working class.

Railway companies quickly realized that they had the seating, the electricity, and the attention of the townsfolk. They could arrange interesting stops for their passengers—more riders, more profit!

Amusement parks did not require great outlays of money for the railways or big expenditures for visitors. A nickel or dime ticket to ride included most activities. The entertainment was for all, old and young, the working class and the emerging leisure class. At the center of trolley park entertainment was music: music of visiting vaudeville acts, music for dancing, music that set a festive atmosphere. There were giant swings, baseball fields, restaurants, a casino, dance halls, and at almost every trolley park found in Maine...a band stand.

Visitors in their best fill trolleys at The Square, York Beach.

Riverton Park, Portland

About four miles from Portland, on the sloping hillside along the Presumpscot River, a summer resort opened on June 20, 1896 to a throng of 10,000 visitors. The Portland Railroad Company, with the assistance of Boston landscape artist Frank M. Blaisdell, spared no expense in the design of this handsome park. Steamers and scores of sailboats departed from Riverton's spacious wharf to take visitors up or down the Presumpscot for a few hours' sail. The park's rustic theatre seated several thousands and featured excellent performers. Its banquet hall sported a dance floor above; a menagerie of fox, deer, elk, and moose were enclosed within fences—and of course, there was a band stand:

> **A grand band-stand or orator's pavilion has been placed in the open grounds for those who wish to utilize it for anything of this kind.**

All was entirely free for those who patronized the electric cars and paid only the normal street fare.

Today, although Riverton's turn-of-the century pleasures are just a memory, walking tours of the area are available in the summertime.

Riverton Park: The band stand was one of the earliest structures built here, as shown in this photo c. 1898.

Riverton Park at the peak of its popularity. This popular destination operated as a trolley park until 1925 and continued as an amusement park until 1929.

Quamphegan Amusement Park

In York County by the late 1800s people no longer used the river for travel; trolleys were king. It was possible to ride all the way from York to Biddeford without even changing cars. When going through South Berwick, trolleys left the Salmon Falls Bridge on the hour, went to the South Berwick Trolley Junction near today's Dover–Eliot Bridge on Route 101, and continued on to Dover and Kittery.

Along this trolley line, in operation from 1900–1922, between South Berwick Junction and the South Berwick Car Barn, was the Quamphegan Amusement Park. Tourists were enticed to visit this park where there were rustic walks, picnic areas, concessions, summerhouses, a merry-go-round ... and the always popular band stand.

Entrance to Quamphegan Park, South Berwick, Me.

The trolley granted access to the music and gaiety at Quamphegan Trolley Park as well as transport to work at the textile mills.

"Quamphegan" is a Native American word meaning "great fishing place."

Riverside Park, Hampden

Many trolley resorts were located just beyond the 5¢ fare limit. This meant carrying passengers to these entertainment centers happily doubled trolley company receipts! This was the case when Riverside Park opened on June 15, 1898. The Hampden, Bangor, and Winterport Electric Company—precursor of the Bangor Hydro Electric Company—operated this 10-acre summer attraction on the Penobscot River. It was a 30-minute ride from Bangor and the 10¢ fare included admission to use the bowling alley and dance hall; see live alligators in special pools; watch silent movies; enjoy traveling vaudeville shows, magicians and acrobats; and celebrate the end of the day with a firework display!

Not far from the popular giant swings was a tall band stand.

Hampden: Giant swings like these at Riverside Park were a popular feature of many trolley parks. Some were even located indoors. (Photo courtesy Richard Newcomb)

Island Park, Winthrop

> **The name evokes summers past. Talk to one or six or a dozen people. Ask what they think of when they hear the phrase "Island Park." Dancing, girls, bootleg whiskey, big bands!**
>
> – Kennebec Journal Historical Series, II, July 3, 1976

The island, owned by the Hersey family, was signed over on July 24, 1902 to the Augusta, Winthrop, and Gardiner Electric Line, which was looking to increase its ridership. They had already constructed another trolley park in the area: Oak Woods Park, in nearby Augusta.

This new summer business was primarily a picnic/swimming area. After you crossed the newly built footbridge, there were swingsets and a bathhouse. From there you ascended the hill, passing a refreshment stand and a band stand. Beyond was the building that became Central Maine's biggest summer attraction: a 150 foot by 75 foot dance pavilion! Island Park's band stand was built around a flag pole, much like the early one at Stockholm.

The summer theatre here burned in 1930 and the park's last days were in the 1940s.

Island Park: The band stand at Cobbseecontee Lake (or "Cobbosee" as it was more commonly known) was overshadowed by the gigantic dance pavilion, to its right.

Island Park, Fairfield

At the southern end of Bunker's Island in Fairfield is a beautiful grove that is now privately owned. The area was once a recreational area known as Island Park. It, too, included a band stand built for entertainers hired to encourage excursions on the "electrics" (trolleys). Amos Gerald, the entrepreneur behind the 1906 Gerald Hotel of Fairfield, Casco Castle of South Freeport, and Brunswick's Merrymeeting Park, owned the trolley line that terminated at Fairfield.

It is believed that the Island Park band stand was built prior to the turn of the century and later removed to railroad property on Lawrence Avenue at the end of Newhall Street. Gerald owned the house across the street at 1 Newhall Street from 1896 to 1900, and the band stand would have formed part of his view from the house's south windows.

Island Park, Fairfield: A rustic band stand that fit very picturesquely into a pine grove.

Oakland Park, Rockport

A ticket on The Rockland, Thomaston, and Camden Street Railway gave you admission to 72-acre Oakland Park, built in 1902. A day's outing here would surely have included baseball—"Trolley Leagues" provided fast, entertaining games. Walking along the pond would also be on the agenda, as of course would be a concert at the square band stand.

Oakland Park was where Rockland folks came for entertainment. The musical heritage of this community included concerts as early as 1856, featuring 6-year-old pianist Carrie Burpee. Later, folks came to hear "Uncle Jimmie"—James Wight, composer of "The Twentieth Century Festival March" (1901) and "The Maine Festival March" (1904). Wight was bandmaster and conductor of the Old Rockland Band before the Civil War and returned to reorganize it later, although the band never achieved its earlier acclaim.

Local historian Barbara F. Dyer, 90, recalls her sister and her boyfriend taking her to a dance at Oakland Park when she was 15. How impressed she was with the "ball of mirrors constantly revolving, sending spots of color all around the dance floor." Later the dance hall turned into a roller-skating rink. Her research also showed that this trolley line had

only two accidents ... in 39 years. One happened August 12, 1911, when Car #22 carrying school children to Warren after a day at Oakland Park met Car #17 head on near O'Brian's siding in Warren. The accident killed one person and injured six more. The explanation given was "a misunderstanding of orders given by the railway superintendent."

Two unusual stone pillars resembling lighthouses marked the entrance to this seaside park. The trolley service ended in 1939 and Howard Dearborn purchased the site, which continues to be run as a motel and cabins.

ENTRANCE TO OAKLAND PARK, ROCKLAND ME

Oakland Park, unlike most Maine trolley parks, was situated by the ocean. Most others were located along a lake or river.

Oakland Park at Rockport beckoned with a summer day's relaxation, just a 15-minute ride from Rockland on the railway. (Photo courtesy Barbara F. Dyer)

The small, roofless band stand at Locke(s) Mills was moved from its site on the other side of the Little Androscoggin River where it serves as a landmark for ALA motorists. Its presence here was short-lived, however; in 1919 while celebrating the end of World War I, exuberant revelers set it on fire.

Band Stands' Last Hurrah:
Driving to Band Stands "In My Merry Oldsmobile"

In 1911, the highway system was in its infancy.

> Only a small part of the people of Maine (are) in automobiles, less than three percent, and only a very small portion of these who do use automobiles will be able to travel very much on the trunk line of highways.
> — unidentified newspaper clipping

Routing via Band Stands

Automobile travelers found mostly "fair dirt and gravel roads with some macadam," and there were few directional signs. Color-coded poles along the roadside, set in place by various trail organizations, provided the only routing assistance. Enter automobile clubs. In 1910, the Maine Automobile Association was formed to share motoring experiences. MAA sent a road book to every member of the association as well as to every "automobilist" who applied for one. These books described the road conditions and often used band stands as landmarks in their awkwardly worded directions:

96.4	2.0 Athens At reverse fork keep straight on over bridge. At road to left beyond, with band stand on right keep straight on, and at fork at large white house called Elmwood Lawn, KEEP LEFT.

Between 1912 and 1914 the Maine Automobile Association saw membership increase from 247 to around 3,000. The organization expended more than $10,000 in a single year, principally on behalf of "good roads propaganda." They laid out and signed detours, and warned towns that they would be held responsible for damage that occured to cars or individuals on dangerous sections of roads. AAA vowed to do greater work in the future.

Despite the United States' entry into World War I in 1917, automobile ownership continued to expand and change Maine village centers. Between 1920 and 1929, the number of vehicles registered nationally jumped from 8 to 23 million, and another Maine auto club, ALA (American Legal Association) was actively publishing touring books. Their Green Books also used band stands as well as trolley lines as identifying markers. For example, in the 1920 edition of the Green Book, the route from Bangor to Calais via Hancock reads:

37.3	Ferry across the Sullivan River Fare 55 cent for roadsters: $1.10 for touring cars
64.3	Cherryfield...turn right through the covered bridge
126.00	Pembroke three Corners: band stand ahead: curve slightly left past post office.

Automobiles were no longer just the toys of the wealthy. As the cost went down, cars themselves became recreational outlets. Soon roadsters replaced the trolley. Sadly, noisy automobiles made it hard to listen to band stand music; trolleys had been much quieter. Buses soon added to the clamor. Noise, as well as other reasons, prompted the relocation and reconfiguration of parks. New settings were designed for strolling and offered laborers welcome relief from the noise and pace of busy mills and quarries. Scenic groves and more isolated park areas removed from clamor became popular places to build or relocate a band stand.

The road from Portland to the New Hampshire Line near Gorham (via Bethel) was designated by banded poles painted yellow and known as the Longfellow Route. This helped the inexperienced traveler find the way. The route went by way of Locke's Mills, once an important crossroads, where a roofless band stand stood behind the railway station. Like many early band stands it had been moved "over the wooden bridge that spanned the "Little Androscoggin River." ALA directions, 1919, mention the band stand, even spelling it using the latest one-word fashion:

36.9	Locke's Mills. Bandstand on left: straight ahead, keeping left at Y just beyond, shortly passing church and cemetery.
42.1	Bethel. After crossing railroad, turn right (for the center of the town keep straight ahead 0.5 mile). Bethel Inn Maple Inn Herrick Brothers Garage

Lost motorists were probably frustrated to find that the band stand burned down in the fire of 1919!

Scrambling to Adjust to the Auto

Maine's love affair with the automobile spread rapidly, reaching even the northernmost regions. In Edward Wiggins's *History of Aroostook* (1922), the author notes that

> **Probably nowhere else in the United States is there a section of equal population where automobiles so abound as in Aroostook. And in the multitude of cars, the great majority are not moderate priced cars, but high-class and pretentious ones. As a natural consequence of the gait it has struck in number and price of cars, garages and gasoline stations are more numerous in Aroostook than saloons used to be in the thirstiest cities before prohibition wiped them from the map and they are**

Creative artwork decorated the advertising in this 1914 AAA tourbook.

The Modern Auto Park

Entrepeneurs sought to cash in on roadster travelers by creating destinations similar to trolley parks. One such attraction was the Carmel Auto Rest Park, built and operated from the 1920s through the 1950s.

Henry Wise purchased the property in 1928. This imaginative proprietor saw the unstoppable growth of the automobile, and the need for gasoline stations, as a way to make money. Soon the Auto Rest Park became a haven for tired motorists and a sure-fire attraction. "Concrete Road All the Way!" proclaimed advertisements for the park. The box of snakes first used to attract tourists grew into a menagerie that included peacock, elk, and pheasant. Before long, monkeys were added, and on special occasions the baby bear cubs were taken out for a romp on leashes. There were cabins, a restaurant, 28 flavors of ice cream, and, of course, a band stand. Amateur talent shows were a big draw and many locals still remember "Yodeling Slim Clark" as a favorite performer.

The Auto Rest Park had famous and infamous visitors. Among the famous were Gene Tunney and bandleader Stan Kenton. The most infamous had to be Al Brady, FBI Public Enemy Number One! The story goes that on October 11, 1937, three well-dressed men spent the night at the cabins in Carmel. They likely played penny poker but never opened the bedclothes. The next day, Brady and company headed to Bangor to pick up some guns, but the FBI was waiting. Two of the murderers were shot dead and the other sang to the authorities!

The Brady incident made national news but Carmel's fame didn't last long. Soon after, the construction of I-95 rerouted traffic and by the mid-1960s this one-stop entertainment center was gone...but not forgotten.

Carmel: Famous for its 28 flavors of ice cream; infamous for the Brady incident!

not only more numerous but are more costly and elaborate, and have a larger patronage than ever saloons had. Assume that Aroostook were wide open alcoholically speaking on no holiday of the year would so many gallons of grogs be poured down.

By 1923 automobiles were even bypassing Portland's finest trolley parks. Riverton changed its name to Riverton Amusement Park and struggled along until 1928. Meanwhile entrepreneurs with vision offered new attractions for motorized travelers. They built handy roadside services: overnight cabins, gasoline stations, and parks made not for strolling but for showing off that new auto!

At Stanwood Park in Farmington, visionaries went a step farther, offering accommodations for guests *and* for automobiles: "eleven garages – private parking places" separated by chicken wire! Visitors could enjoy "The Booth," a tearoom that served ice cream and candy. Of course, there was also the band stand and nearby pony rides. Stanwood Park went into decline during the war years and closed sometime in the 1940s.

As the last new band stands were being built at auto parks in the 1920s, many were already being torn down to make room for expanded highway construction. The Great War and the flu epidemic were over, women had won the vote, Prohibition was law, and traveling by automobile was the modern way to go. Fewer and fewer people visited the elaborate trolley parks built at the end of the last century. Leisure activities were changing fast: radios, phonographs, and movies were all the rage. Large halls, made accessible by the growing number of autos, were built for the new dance music sounds, and speakeasies were the new gathering place. The band stand era came to an end as Maine's population moved inside.

Stanwood Park, Farmington: A "herd" of automobiles surrounds the popular band stand in this image from the 1920s.

A big attraction at Stanwood was "the largest zoo in the state." The menagerie started with bear cubs and soon expanded to include monkeys, lions, buffalo, deer, and more.

New businesses now occupy the Stanwood Park site. The greenhouse for Strawberry Fields Nursery was once part of Stanwood, as was a newly opened teahouse. On its wooden floor, oil spills can still be seen!

BAND STANDS
Tell Their Stories

A Selection of Maine Band Stands

Each town and every location where a band stand once stood has a unique story to tell. Some are well documented, others remain as a single line in a history book or as a memory recalled by the town's eldest resident during an evening of reminiscences.

Maine in the late 1800s, with its sparsely populated areas, could be a remote and lonely place. At a time when Britain was building Victorian "pagodas" in urban parks where city dwellers could go to escape the crush of industry and teeming humanity, Maine was building band stands to encourage townsfolk to gather together, socialize, and make music.

Reflecting on the building of individual Maine band stands allows us to see how band stand history is embedded in the social history of each town. So now, let's begin.

Ashland: The message on the back of this postcard reads "This is the band stand and some of the crowd that was here last Sunday and a big day we had." It was mailed August 27, 1937 to New Bedford, Massachusetts. On the side of the building can be seen both U.S. and Canadian flags.

Ashland: *Useful and unique*

County: Aroostook
Construction Date: 1937
Builder/Designer: Charles Carter, Band Leader
Current Location: Corner of Plumb Street, behind elementary school
Description: First story 20' square; second story 18' octagon

THE ASHLAND BAND STAND WAS A LATE ADDITION to Maine's band stand roster, built at the time when many of Maine's original old band stands were beginning to disappear. It was of a unique design: a traditional octagonal band stand on the second floor, surmounted a 20' square first floor building!

Charles A. Carter, a carpenter by trade, designed and built Ashland's band stand. Carter joined the Ashland town band in 1883 at the age of 14 as an E-flat cornet player. Fifty-two years later, in 1935, he organized the Ashland Military Band Association and remained its leader for eleven more years. His tenure certainly gave him first-hand experience of what features an Ashland band stand should have, and in 1937, after 54 years as a band musician, he started construction.

By then the country was in the midst of the Great Depression. However, the town still had reason for fanfare, and the band stand was built for the occasion of Ashland's Centennial Celebration. Afterwards, the town appropriately dedicated the structure to Carter, the man who had played in their summer concerts, marched in their parades, and taught so many young musicians—

> ... the leader who had worked untiring with the band and its members to secure the band stand ...

Carter's band stand design allowed band members a lofty visibility for the large crowds that came to listen to the weekly concerts. When not in use, the drop panels on the upper floor could be closed to protect the structure from harsh winters, and the first story of the building was heated and made a fine place to rehearse or to store instruments! Both features were immensely practical for a northern Maine town with lots of heavy weather. (Speaking of practicality, word has it that some Massachusetts band stands had "comfort stations" located on the first floor! This was not the case in Ashland.)

The band stand was originally located closer to Exchange Street. In the early 1940s it was moved by a team of horses to a newly purchased lot, which is its present location.

In 1987, the band stand was renovated, and on July 9th, during Ashland's Sesquicentennial Week, a special Music Day was held to celebrate the town's interesting musical history. Maine Speaker of the House John L. Martin spoke, and of course the Ashland Community Band played.

The Ashland Area Business Association is revitalizing this band stand once again. The town celebrated the summer of 2001 with an "Ashland Daze Festival." The Business Association opened the second story panels on the band stand, hung "Old Glory" for all to see, and floodlit the flag to honor and celebrate the 4th of July.

A pewter coin (left) was minted to celebrate the Sesquicentennial rededication of Ashland's band stand in 1987. It was similar to one that was made for the Union Bicentennial in 1974 (right).

Athens: *Liberated ladies*

County: Franklin
Construction Date: 1904
Builder: Unknown; built for town centennial celebration
Current Location: Wesserunsett Valley Fairgrounds
 (Route 150, South Main Street)
Description: Small, 11', has been renovated

THE YEAR WAS 1904 when Evelyn went to the Athens Post Office and mailed two postcards to her friend Miss Nina Candage at Seal Harbor. This was long before Athens had many modern amenities—telephones, phonographs, or automobiles. Evelyn's postcard did show, though, that Athens had a town band, outfitted in resplendent uniforms!

Even more unusual, Athens had a Ladies Band—at a time when "ladies" were much more likely to be found in the parlor seated primly at the piano! There is little record of other "All Ladies Bands" at this time in Maine history, although Helen May Butler, from New Hampshire, had organized and led the first Ladies' Military Band in Providence, Rhode Island, in 1873. Women more frequently served as accompanists to men and only occasionally did they direct bands.

From Evelyn's choice of postcards we learn a lot about Athens' musical scene. Not only did this town have a fine band stand and a proudly uniformed cornet band of at least 18 members, but their band appears to have had a woman (back row, left) and a very young boy (second row, center). They must have been regular performers, as they are fully arrayed in band uniforms.

The year of Athens' Centennial was 1904. It had not been an easy year for the town; Somerset Academy had caught fire and was so badly damaged that school could not be held for a month. On June 9, 1904, though, money was found to start work on the pavilion that was to be used at the Centennial—and also on the bandstand.

The band stand is still in use. It has been moved twice: first, from the spot where it was built, presently the location of the Trueworthy Bungalow, and then to the Ellingwood field about across from the Grange Hall. Later it was moved to its present site at the Wesserunsett Valley Fair Grounds. The present band stand however, looks lower and larger than the earlier pictures.

Athens: The band is ready to perform in honor of Governor's Day at the Fairgrounds in Athens.

Athens: Marching *with a sign* "Athens Band, 1904," this liberated group (below) felt no need to proclaim themselves a "Ladies Band." They had as many members as the Athens Cornet Band (right, joined by a woman and a young boy), but what were their instruments?

Bangor: *Musical city*

County: Penobscot
Construction Date: Five known band stands with different dates
Builder: See individual descriptions
Locations, Descriptions: See text below

BANGOR, "THE QUEEN CITY," WAS THE LARGEST MUNICIPALITY east of the Kennebec River and had a reputation of being the "most musical city of its size in America."

It was Melville H. Andrews (1845–1921), leader of the 12th Maine Regiment Band during the Civil War, who brought march music home to Bangor. Andrews was a talented violin and cello player who composed patriotic songs such as "Pride of the Army" and "Pride of the Navy." It is noted that at the conclusion of the War, officers presented him with a silver cornet.

Andrews went on to establish the Andrews Music House, a business that sponsored many gifted local composers, including R.B. Hall, who dedicated his first march composition—"M.H.A." to his mentor.

In 1867, Andrews organized the small but well respected Andrews Orchestra in Bangor. From this group and its successor, Pullen's Orchestra, the present Bangor Symphony was developed. In fact, Andrews conducted the BSO from December 1901 until 1904.

The Bangor Band is the second oldest continuously operating band in the country. In its heyday the group was in such demand that it played twice a week, fifty weeks a year! If their schedule truly indicates the ciy's love of music, it is not surprising that Bangor's parks were all outfitted with their own individual band stands. What is surprising is the lack of pictures documenting these band stands!

BROADWAY PARK
Bounded by French and Pine Streets between North and South Park Street, Broadway was one of the earliest parks established in Bangor and was a forerunner of the post Civil War movement to create urban green spaces. This band stand is noted on the 1874–1875 Bangor Atlas, but the band stand was likely not built until the 1890s. It stood close to South Park, halfway between Broadway and French Streets.

UNION PARK
This was a small square located behind the landmark Bangor House, bounded by May, Summer, and Union Streets. The hotel is said to have hosted six presidents: Grant, Arthur, Benjamin Harrison, McKinley, Theodore Roosevelt, and Taft. Could some of them have enjoyed the band stand here?

CHAPIN PARK
In 1898, Bangor Park Commissioners approved a plan from Frank Blaisdell, a Boston landscape architect and civil engineer who worked on several Maine parks, including Portland's Riverton Trolley Park and Merrymeeting Trolley Park in Brunswick. Plans called for Bangor to have the "handsomest of them all" with a band stand, pool, fountain, seats, walkways, and plantings to be built at the City Common Bangor, later to be called Forest Avenue Park. The park's band stand was close to the Coombs Street (formerly Fulton Row) end of the park. Later this area would be renamed Chapin Park after Mayor Arthur Chapin presented the city with a special decorative fountain.

DAVENPORT PARK
This small, beautifully landscaped park was the place for band stand concerts in the 1940s. Bob Jones, a drummer with the Bangor Band, recalls his uniform as "light blue with sand brown belts and shoulder baldrics. We had a lot of fun with these since we could easily be mistaken for troopers." The musicians would raise havoc by going out and comically directing traffic!

The park was developed on land donated in 1898 at the end of the Spanish American War by Isaac Davenport. A brass shield and scrollwork from the bow of the USS Maine, sunk in Havana Harbor in February 1898, was erected here as a memorial. It still remains as a focal point; the bow scroll was recently refurbished. Unfortunately, Davenport's band stand, where the Bangor Band used to perform in concert, no longer exists.

Central Park

The band stand here, sited at nearby Market Square between Harlow and Central Streets, cost $325 when it was erected by H. L. Jewel in 1881. Because of its location, comfortable seats, and velvety lawn, it was the most renowned of all Bangor's band stands. It has been described as "an octagonal band stand, the platform on a high base and with Italianate posts supporting a slightly everted pointed roof topped by a finial." The Center Park band stand was likely burned in the Bangor fire of 1911.

Bangor musicians Greg Osgood and Woody Woodman remember the musical heyday of the late 1940s in Bangor but doubt that the city had any band stands then. Instead, the City provided a portable stage with interlocking platforms for the Bangor bands, which played a series of concerts at city parks on a rotating basis. These platforms were equipped with upright columns for lighting and could be easily disassembled and moved to the site of the next concert.

Another former Bangor band member who searched his memory was Bill Stetson of the Penobscot Wind Ensemble. He recalled another band stand across the street from Bangor's Public Library (in the 1930s, near Murray Motor Lot). Does anyone else remember this location?

This Bangor park (top right) is often referred to as Center, Centre, or Central Park. The early stereoview shown here was made before the trees obscured the band stand.

The Spanish American Soldier's and Sailors' Monument (right) in Davenport Park. The park's band stand is set under a bower of trees.

On summer evenings in Bar Harbor, local families and tourists still gather on the village green in the shadow of the Bar Harbor Congregational Church to listen to the town band. (Photo and permission for reproduction courtesy Ed Elvidge)

Bar Harbor: *and the Boston Symphony*

County: Hancock
Construction Date: 1899
Builder: Unknown
Current Location: Village Green, Main and Mount Desert Streets
Description: Rebuilt

IT WAS CUSTOMARY IN BAR HARBOR for the boys to run around the band stand in one direction, while a group of giggling girls circled the other way. It was also customary, if not widely acknowledged, for couples to snuggle out of sight behind the band stand!

Bar Harbor's band stand became a reality when, just before the turn of the century, the Town bought the property that had previously been the site of the Grand Central Hotel complex for the sum of $45,000. The hotel was torn down and the lot cleaned up. Eighty-nine dollars was raised to build a band stand on the vacant lot. This was not enough money to complete the job, so an additional $40 was raised in order for the first concert to be held on July 21, 1899. The band members were pleased: they would no longer sit on chairs scattered on the ground!

A few years later the village green was saved from becoming the site of a new grammar school. Excavation had already begun when a new town meeting rescinded the decision and it was decided instead to build the school on Ledgelawn Avenue.

In "A Native's Memories of Old Bar Harbor" in *Down East Magazine*, September 1970, Nan Cole described the band of the early 1900s as:

> ... local musicians, each pridefully aware both of his talent and his bandsman's uniform. The dark blue suits, trimmed with gold braid were topped by blue-visored caps, and the brass buttons on the uniforms, as well as each man's shoes and band instruments, all were polished to a high luster that gleamed in the lights from the bandstand.

It also recalled that:

> The players had entered the stand by means of a ladder, which, once they were ensconced, was stored beneath the platform until the concert was over.

The question of who should perform at the band stand was so controversial that a packed town meeting was convened at the Casino to discuss the matter. Should the Boston Symphony replace the local band to provide "better" music for the rusticators? A compromise offered by a Matron of the Eastern Star allowed that the local band would play four evenings a week and the Boston Symphony the remaining three. This idea found favor and for many years 30 members of the Symphony played at Bar Harbor.

In 1920 the Village Improvement Association sought the assistance of longtime summer colony member and distinguished landscape gardener Beatrix Farrand regarding the beautification of the green. She had studied under Charles Sprague Sargent, director of the Arnold Arboretum, and achieved such an outstanding reputation that in 1899 she joined Frederick L. Olmsted, Sr. and Frederick L. Olmsted, Jr. as the only woman founder of the American Institute of Landscape Architects. Farrand, who was working locally with the Rockefeller family on landscaping the carriage roads of Acadia National Park, advised the town to alter the concept for the village green, banish the barberry hedges, and move the band stand (then located closer to the center of the park) to a location closer to the north side.

This was done. The band stand has remained at the site despite a movement to relocate it back to its original spot when the structure was rebuilt in 1972. In the 1990s it was once again rebuilt and remains a popular site of summer concerts.

Souvenir items featuring the band stand were hand-painted in Germany and sold at shops such as "The Little Store" in Bar Harbor, now part of the current shop at 85 Main Street. (Courtesy Susan Fox-Jackson)

Bath: *A Victorian park*

County: Sagadahoc
Construction Date: c. 1889
Builder: Francis Fassett, Park Superintendent John H. Ramsay
Original Location: Lincoln Park, Washington and Summer Streets
Description: Large with red/pink roof

PICTURE BATH'S CITY PARK AS IT WAS in the early 20th century. Early postcards show a pond with boulders along the edges, a fountain, and a rustic bridge. The band stand, with its "startling variety of colors" (its roof was pinkish-red) was built in 1883 and occupied a prominent place in the newly landscaped Victorian-style park.

Unlike most Maine band stands built by local carpenters or band members, this one had a well-renowned designer, Francis Fassett, who was also the architect responsible for Portland's Baxter Building (formerly the Portland Public Library) on Congress Street.

Bath's band stand was one of many features of the park plan envisioned by John Ramsay, Bath's Superintendent of Cemeteries from 1883 to 1897 and a landscape gardener. The property on which the band stand was constructed was formerly the home of Peleg Tallman (1764–1840), a naval hero and prominent businessman. The fruit trees that surrounded his home were replaced with shade trees and the property enclosed with a fence. One account described the park as being transformed from "a pasture to a beauty spot."

By the 1940s the park pool and fountain were in dismal condition. The sculptor William Zorach agreed to design a new fountain, and the Bath Garden Club raised the necessary funds. The bronze casting, "Spirit of the Sea" by William Zorach was in place by August of 1962 —but like many sculptures, it was not without its critics!

The Patten Free Library was built in 1889, the same year as the band stand. It was therefore appropriate, when the Library celebrated its 100th birthday in 1989, that a new "gazebo" be built on the site left empty when the band stand was torn down in 1953. Though not the same, James Stilphen's design is reminiscent of the earlier style. Its imposing size—34 feet in diameter with double staircases—and its prominent location bring a wonderful sense of community to Bath.

Musical Bath: Bath's beautiful new band stand (bottom photo), modeled after the older 1889 band stand (top photo), is often home to the Bath Municipal Band, formed in 1961. This busy group attracts musicians from 20 or more surrounding towns and owns a building with a rehearsal hall, kitchen, and library, not to mention its own portable band stand! The band has played for ship launchings at Bath Iron Works, shared a platform with the U. S. Marine Band, and is always a hit at R. B. Hall Day celebrations.

Calais: *Music—an international affair*

County: Washington
Construction Date: c. 1900
Builder: Unknown
Current Location: Memorial Park
Description: Earlier, had a bass drum extension

THE IMPRESSIVE BAND STAND AT CALAIS was, of necessity, one of the largest in Maine. This city hosted an international band with representatives from Calais and Milltown, Maine as well as St. Stevens and Milltown, New Brunswick. This town was so in love with music that at one point it boasted eight bands! Calais band members would fill in at Woodland when that town was without a band and often went to Eastport to play with the Indian Band. As many as 30 or 40 musicians stood ready to play some of the more difficult band overtures composed, drawing from a large selection of sheet music brought home in a trunk after World War I by Frank Billing. Some music was so difficult that one frustrated band member was heard to exclaim:

The fellow that wrote that couldn't play it himself!

When the band broke up after World War II, band member Ken McLaine took home the music collection and the band's bass drums. Tragically, all was lost when his house caught fire.

In 2000, Harry Lewis, age 94, reminisced about the great days of the Calais bands, and the memory of the bass drums brought out a story.

On a summer night, the boys in the band were shooting the breeze on the sidewalk waiting for practice to begin. ... Along came a big hound dog, who lifted his leg and dropped about a quart, right in the bass drum!

Lewis recalled playing with Ernest Fountain, a slide trombonist for John Philip Sousa. Sousa played his last tour in 1928 at St. John, New Brunswick, and the Calais Band was on hand for the event! Harry also remembered a British man from the English Army Band, and Bernie Francis, a saxophonist who played the minstrel circuit.

Calais: The band stand was part of the town's Memorial Park plan. A Union Soldier Monument was dedicated in 1898 to "People who lost lives, 1861–1865." A fountain was dedicated in 1909. As large as the band stand was, it was still too small for Calais' large band population. An extension (at left in photo) had to be added for the bass drum!

Calais' current band stand (right) has been renovated several times (even resurrected after a fire), and still hosts concerts at Memorial Park.

Cape Elizabeth: *The band stands of Fort Williams*

County: Cumberland
Construction Date: See below
Builder: Civil Conservation Corp (1937 band stand)
Original Location: Fort Williams band stands— Using the *Fort Williams Walking Guide*, the 1909 band stand is #78, 1911 is #73, and the 1937 band stand is #58. Bowery Beach band stand: date unknown; Cape Cottage Casino band stand, Surf Road: c. 1898

At Fort Williams, a narrative panel tells the history of dozens of structures ranging from an ammunition bunker to a band stand. The oldest band stand (1909) renovated in 1965, remains standing near the high promontory of Portland Head Light and is weighted down with four large concrete slabs. Never could it be blown out to sea!

As part of the Fort's original plan, band members were quartered in their own barracks, the last building on Barracks Row, near Shore Road. The group's popularity is manifested by the construction of a second band stand, located northeast of the original structure in 1911.

Concerts by The Coast Artillery Band were well-attended events. When the famous Fifth Infantry Regiment returned from Germany in 1922, it was stationed at Portland Harbor. So many of the soldiers were discharged and the vacancies then filled with Maine recruits that

> **the Maine Stein Song was adopted as the official regimental marching song!**
>
> – *Portland Head Light & Fort Williams*, Kenneth E. Thompson Jr.

The band was honored to play at many well-attended events, including Portland's first (December 1924) radio broadcast on WCSH. In 1939 they were deployed to the Panama Canal.

In 1937 in the midst of the Great Depression, Fort Williams served as an induction center for the Civilian Conservation Corps. CCC workers constructed a third band stand at Fort Williams—a simple, round concrete-walled platform that still exists northwest of the original band stand. Lenora Bangert, a former Fort Williams employee, recalls that the CCC crew always had a picnic in this band stand at cleanup time. (Lenora was Fort Williams' first female civilian worker. The military were unprepared for her; when she first reported for work on December 7, 1940, there was no desk or typewriter—only a seat in the hall. She persevered, and was the Fort's last employee out when the Army declared the fort "excess to military needs" in 1963.)

The earliest Fort Williams band stand was used by Governor John H. Reed when he spoke from its platform to honor Cape Elizabeth during the town's Bicentennial celebration in 1965. The structure was later reconstructed, with roof improvements estimated to cost $25,000 in 1979. Oddly, a good photo exists of this band stand in a conference room at the Doubletree Hotel, Portland.

Music in Cape Elizabeth was not confined to Fort Williams. A band flourished for a time at Town House Corner known as the Town House Band; the group took their inspiration from Merrimen's Band of South Portland. Under the instruction of Frank Collins, a prominent local bandsman, and directed by Philip Robinson, they practiced their spirited music until a band stand was built specifically for them to give summer concerts at Bowery Beach (now Crescent Beach).

At Fort Williams: The Fifth Infantry Regiment Band was an 80-piece, high-class concert band.

Fort Williams, 1930s: Throngs of spectators arrived by automobile sometime in the 1930s, some watching the soldiers drill from the Fort's second (1911) band stand. This one, now gone, is visible at the upper center of the photo. (Both photos courtesy Kenneth E. Thompson, Jr.)

Damariscotta: *Fire protection*

County: Lincoln
Construction Date: c. 1895
Builder: Unknown
Original Location: Bristol Road and Business Route 1
Description: Hexagon

OCTAGON-SHAPED HOUSES, INTRODUCED IN THE 1850s AND 1860s, found limited favor in Maine. The shape did, however, offer advantages for a band stand: visibility without any dark, useless corners, exposure to cross ventilation, and ample visibility to see, as well as hear, band concerts. The eight-sided structure became the most prevalent, but not the only shape found in Maine.

Damariscotta had one of the few known examples of a hexagon-shaped band stand (it appears from early pictures of Lewiston's City Park that their earliest band stand was also of a hexagon shape).

Damariscotta did not build its six-sided band stand solely for music and entertainment. After several devastating fires in which firefighters ran short of water, an article appeared on the 1893 Town Warrant to see what might be done to ensure fire protection and water supply. *The History of the Massasoit Engine Company* reports that "a large tank was put in the ground on the Common, and $150 appropriated to pay for the work. A pipe led across the street so that street sprinklers could be filled when dust was prevalent. A band stand of the same circumference was erected over the top of the water tank."

At a later, undetermined date the little triangle in front of the Baptist Church was improved with a new band stand that remained at the triangle until 1933, when it was removed and the water tank floored over for continued use. Word has it this was done because the road was being widened, leaving little room for the band stand. Harold Castener moved it to his home a few doors down on Bristol Street where it became his garden "gazebo."

This triangle retained another feature: the town's historic cannon, which had been placed on the green during the 1930s. The story of this famous cannon—a small, 42-inch gun with a 37-inch bore—was reported in the *Lincoln County News*. The account identifies it as one of the British cannons secretly dragged in a 300-day cross-country journey during the winter blizzards of 1776 from Fort Ticonderoga, New York to Dorchester Heights in Boston. The artillery was used on May 17, when British troops were astonished to be fired upon by their own cannons and had to evacuate Boston. The engineer of this feat of transportation was Maine's Henry Knox, who was appointed General of the Continental army, and later, Secretary of War under Washington.

The cannon was subsequently brought to Damariscotta by Captain Jeremiah Knowlton on one of this sailing voyages. When Grover Cleveland defeated James G. Blaine of Maine for the U. S. Presidency in 1884, local Democrats, including Maurice Mulligan, borrowed the cannon from Mr. Knowlton, set it on a high knoll back of the village, loaded it with three pounds of powder and fired it off. The cannon kicked so hard that it buried itself in the ground and was lost for about two years.

In 1886, Mr. Knowlton wanted some dry wood, which he purchased from Mr. James Mulligan. When his son Maurice hauled it over, "Knowlton ... inquired about the cannon and Maurice told him he knew where it was and Mr. Knowlton said he would like to have it back. He went over with an ox cart and dug it out and hauled it back to his place on Round Top.... Here it stayed until the triangle was improved with a new bandstand and someone got permission to get the cannon and place it on the green there." *(see more cannon stories on page 132).*

The cannon still graces the triangle that once teemed with activity, especially during firemen's musters. Advance preparation was, of course, essential before the big competition and the muster team would block off the street and practice near the Baptist Church. Firemen would load young boys on the hand pumper to increase the weight. The goal was to shoot the water over the church roof!

Damariscotta: The town built this charming hexagon-shaped band stand to cover the water tank that not only provided fire protection but was used to sprinkle the dusty streets in summer.

Dixfield: *New uses for old band stands*

County: Oxford
Construction Date: c. 1890
Builder: Unknown
Original Location: See below
Description: Two band stands; see below

East Dixfield: Square and roofless, suitable for recyling!

WILLOW TREES NO LONGER DEFINE THE VILLAGE OF EAST DIXFIELD. Route 2 meanders in such a way that East Dixfield is a village divided between two towns and two counties: one portion is in Wilton (Franklin County) and part in Dixfield (Oxford County). Drivers on Route 2 hurry by the Baptist Church and the remains of a stone wall, never knowing that sometime around 1915, a large square, open band stand complete with electric lighting stood here. Next to it was a stable for boarding the horses of neighbors who came to attend church and social events at this open platform.

Althea Fish remembers when this band stand was "recycled." A building was erected, using the band stand as its foundation, to house Wheelwright's Music Store. This is a fond memory because it was here, Mrs. Fish remembers, that her father Walton bought her mother a piano! Today East Dixfield would seem an unlikely place to locate a music store, but the popularity of piano music in the home is documented. Records in the *Industrial Journal* of May 23, 1884, tell that the town of Dexter had "music furnished by 70 pianos and an as yet uncounted number of parlor organs." Sheet music was even printed in the newspapers. (The band stand was not the only building recycled by the frugal citizens of East Dixfield. The Mystic River Grange was originally constructed in 1893 as a cheese factory.)

The town of Dixfield, originally called Holmantown, also had a band stand on a green area not far from the present location of Towel's Store at the town center. Mrs. Fish remembers the recycling of that band stand too: Arthur Brown Jr. moved it to his house, where it became a garage for his Model A Ford!

Dixfield's first band was organized in 1860. By 1890 the town not only had a band, it had a mission:

To educate the community as well as the band to a better understanding and appreciation of real music.

By 1928 the Dixfield Band possessed a musical library to be proud of. It was valued at nearly $1,000 and included standard arrangements from many of the great composers, old and new. Much of the original music and memorabilia is today at the Dixfield Historical Society.

From the age of 16 (1890), G. Dana Holt was a charter member of the Dixfield Band. This noted musician (cornetist) and conductor was a source of great pride for Dixfield. Holt conducted many concerts in the band stand and was known to have composed an original march for the Sousa Band. He played at the Colonial Theater in Boston as well as with the Boston, Portland, and Bangor Symphony Orchestras. Today, Dixfield's new band stand is named in his honor.

Mr. Holt had two other musical brothers: Hershel and Tom, who was the leader of the school band. Aubrey Kilbreth, a well-remembered drummer, recalls that during his "interning" with the Holts, the band used to march from Dixfield across the Androscoggin River to West Peru every Memorial Day. Some years the wind would blow so hard their music and faded green caps would blow off. Eventually, it got too much for the aging band members to walk. For a while they rode on a Timberland lowbed, but they finally had to give up the windy parade crossing.

Durham: *Saved by a citizen*

County: Androscoggin
Construction Date: c. 1888
Builder: Unknown
Current Location: Intersection of Routes 9 and 136
Description: Small

This small town was at the height of its prosperity prior to 1900. South West Bend was one of Durham's four villages. More business was transacted here than in Lewiston/Auburn. Ladies came to the milliner's shop. Sawmills, gristmills, and even a chair factory were built on its streams. South Bend, on the west side of the Androscoggin, was the location of the town band stand.

Durham's abundant musical talent was represented well by Joseph G. Tyler, born in Pownal. Joe learned to read music while eavesdropping on the music teacher at the schoolhouse where he worked supplying firewood for the stove. By 1844 he was teaching singing and organized the first brass band in nearby Pownal. This one was short lived, but the band he formed in Durham continued for over thirty years.

Another memorable Durham musician was "Uncle Josh" Miller. He could play the snare drum with three sticks at once, keeping one stick in the air and keeping time with the other two!

> **Word has it that "when the Durham band was heard out of doors, the sound caused such a commotion that people fell on their knees and prayed because they thought it was Gabriel's trumpet... (they) ran from their houses bare headed ... and otherwise insufficiently clothed, to see what of seraphim and cherubim was abroad."**
>
> – Coastal Publishing, October 29, 1969

Durham's "cute little band stand" was evident in photos of the 1889 Durham Centennial celebration. If Tyler's Band played there, as is often recalled, this band stand may well date back to the 1870s.

Durham's popularity declined when the railroad from Portland to Auburn agreed to bypass the town. The farmers did not want the noisy trains disturbing their livestock! The highway construction crew, when widening the road, moved the deteriorating band stand out of the way, probably in the 1950s. It sat abandoned and in sad repair until Maxine Herling, fearing that this part of Durham's past would be lost, stopped by the town office to talk about her concern.

Mrs. Herling learned from the selectmen that any citizen was welcome to move the band stand. With their permission, she arranged for a sled and a team of horses, and very carefully, the little band stand was placed at its present location.

There were once two grocery stores at this corner and the band stand is located where a hotel originally stood. The band stand was rededicated in the later 1950s, and since that time Mrs. Herling and her family have cared for and preserved it as a part of Durham's history.

Durham: Straight past the band stand and at the river's edge, one could catch the Androscoggin Ferry to Lisbon. The building on the left was Durham House, later Ford's Hotel; on the right is the store that belonged to Maxine Herling's father. On the river, at the end of Ferry Road, was a corn-processing factory.

Farmington: *"A great ornament"*

County: Franklin
Construction Date: 1874 (Meeting House Park); 1920s–1940s (Stanwood Park)
Architect: Henry Sprague (Meeting House Park)
Current Location: Meeting House Park, Exchange and Main Streets; Stanwood Park, originally on Route 2 (see page 88)

MEETING HOUSE PARK BAND STAND

The "common" at Farmington was described in 1870 as "a receptacle for cows, horses, old carts, etc." but by 1874 it was "a great ornament."

The catalyst for the dramatic change was the organization of the Farmington Cornet Band. With $250 raised by popular subscription, the band purchased instruments by mail. When they arrived, "they were displayed at the home of Hon. J. W. Fairbanks to the satisfaction of all musical people."

In 1874 Henry Sprague built a large wooden band stand measuring $24\frac{1}{2}$ feet across. Today it is considered a treasure, but only two years after its construction, the local paper reported that

> The beautiful common in our village—that should be the pride of all our citizens has been given up, we regret to say, to general neglect, save the portion that have been appropriated by private parties for a lumber and store yard.

By 1886 there were

> decaying trees, unfenced ground, occasional piles of stone and numberless vehicles of as many names (which) tell a story of general neglect—an eyesore upon the village."

– (Maine Olmstead Alliance, Maine Survey)

It was not until 1903, when a wealthy sawmill owner offered to give a Civil War monument to the town if money were spent to beautify the park, that Farmington citizens voted several hundred dollars to improve the property by laying out walks, providing iron seats, etc. In 1904 a monument, of the same design as one erected at Gettysburg in memory of the men of the Sixteenth Maine Infantry, was erected and the band stand moved to an adjacent lot to provide a better view of the monument. At a later date, the band stand was moved back.

Today the "Farmington Common" (Meeting House Park) is again a source of pride in this community. The band stand with its iron fence and fountain, crowned floor, and 14-inch wide benches is now often remembered as the home of band concerts given by the prominent Wheeler's Band under the direction of William F. Miner and the "Old Crows," who are rumored to be named after the liquor of the same name. Apparently, at the band's first parade—Halloween, 1952—a bottle was offered to help some of the older players, dressed as Indians, perform their war dance better!

Farmington: Farmington's monument records that 305 men were sent to fight in the Civil War; 13 were killed, 35 died of disease, and 25 of related injuries. On the town common (now Meeting House or Memorial Park, opposite the Franklin County Court House) stands the oldest of Maine's band stands still in existence. It is also one of the largest, measuring nearly 25 feet across.

Greenville: *Construction or demise?*

County: Piscataquis
Construction Date: c. 1900
Builder: Unknown
Original Location: Near war monument at site of present Union Evangelical Church

GREENVILLE'S EARLY BAND STAND is hard to document. An early postcard, postmarked 1911 (below), shows Union Church (now Union Evangelical Church, United Church of Christ), the old Town Hall next door, and the frame of a band stand. The photo was probably taken a few years earlier, but what about the band stand? Was it just being put up? Taken down? Or in the process of renovation?

The only other photo known to exist shows a completed band stand, but not on any landscaped grounds. Greenville Historical Society members lean toward the theory that this photo is earlier than the photo taken in 1911, when, they feel, the band stand was probably being dismantled. Old timers remember a wooden structure on the spot where the band stand once stood, but it was probably a later structure dating from the World War II era. It preceded the War Memorial built in the 1980s.

In 2001 Greenville constructed and dedicated a new band stand that citizens are rightfully proud to use.

Greenville: The above photo, while unclear, confirms that a roof once topped the Greenville band stand. The photo, left, is believed to have been taken later, when the band stand was being torn down. (Photo courtesy Greenville Historical Society)

107

Harpswell: *A summer community*

County: Sagadahoc
Construction Date: c. 1920
Builder: Unknown
Current Location: South Harpswell, across from Hurricane Ridge Road

SINCE THE 1920S, SOUTH HARPSWELL HAS BEEN HOME to a summer community. At the corner near Hurricane Ridge Road and Route 123 was the Germania Hotel, named after the brass section of Berlin, Germany's large symphonic orchestra, the Germania Serenade Band. These fine musicians escaped the political and religious persecution of the 1850s and brought classical music to the United States, where they were so well received that P.T. Barnum hired them to tour with Jenny Lind, "The Swedish Nightingale." The band toured extensively along the east coast, including Maine. The name "Germania," however, was not in favor once World War II came along; hence the hotel's name change to "The Sea Gables."

The band stand that perched on a rocky point near the hotel has been gone for many years but its location is easy to establish. Still embedded in the wall, though now covered with moss, is an assemblage of seashells collected by a previous owner during his travels.

Harpswell: Hotels added band stands to take advantage of a fine view, as well as provide platforms for local entertainment. This band stand remained for patrons to enjoy a scenic ocean vista even after the Germania Hotel was renamed Sea Gables.

Jefferson: *Lights up!*

County: Lincoln
Construction Date: c. 1910
Builder: Unknown
Current Location: Route 126 near Town Office
Description: Small, 12½' across

Young Basil Achorn at age 8, began playing cornet. By the age of nine he was a regular band member...

EACH SATURDAY, BASIL LEFT HIS HOME IN THE MORNING and bicycled to Winslow Mills (about 8 miles), where he caught the train to Brunswick (about 35 miles). From there, he hopped the trolley (about 20 more miles) to Lewiston—all in order to take his weekly cornet lesson! So records the *Lincoln County News*.

Basil's devotion was surely due in large part to the excellent standards demanded by Jefferson's town band. Organized soon after 1907, when the talented cornetist Harry Morrill came to Jefferson, the new musical group created enough excitement for a small (12½ feet wide) band stand to be built. News clippings tell of

> ... lanterns that hung from the rafters above each bandsman to light his music while Japanese lanterns strung from the posts to surrounding trees added to the festivity.
>
> Concerts prompted folks to travel by horse and buggy and Model T. They flocked to the site from miles around by foot, bicycle, to hear the talented band. ... Despite their protesting elders, children perched on the railing that stood by the road to protect passersby from the steep bank down to the river. Women cranked homemade ice cream and collected money to pay for the band's grand (though overly warm and uncomfortable) dark uniforms.

- *Kennebec Journal*

For many years the band played daily during the Union and Damariscotta Fairs. The musicians disbanded in 1918.

By the 1930s, when the junction of Route 126 and Valley Road was widened, the band stand had been badly neglected and frequently vandalized. Thanks to Forrest Bond, it was taken up to Haskell Mountain and set up near the fire tower. For the most part it remained unused while at this location.

In 1985 under the auspices of the Historical Society, Philip Peaslee moved the band stand from Haskell Mountain. Wooden beams propped in the center provided support and boulders were moved, branches sawed apart, and potholes filled for the move. It took just 2 hours to navigate the narrow dirt road and finally erect the band stand on its present site near the Town Office. Today, it hosts occasional musicians and several weddings and looks especially festive when gaily decorated and floodlit for Christmas.

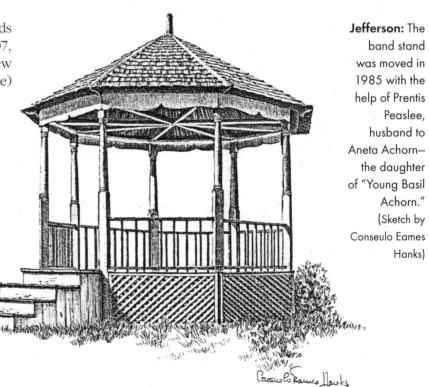

Jefferson: The band stand was moved in 1985 with the help of Prentis Peaslee, husband to Aneta Achorn—the daughter of "Young Basil Achorn." (Sketch by Conseulo Eames Hanks)

Kingfield: *Band stand on the move*

County: Franklin
Construction Date: c. 1897
Builder: Unknown
Current Location: At One Stanley Avenue Restaurant and B&B

"The Kingfield band stand finds a new home"
This headline must have been repeated often in Kingfield's past!

A private mailing card dated 1898 portrays the band stand as the center of attraction near the corner of Main and Depot Streets in this rural village. It started life at the local trotting park but was apparently moved to this corner where it remained for about a decade. Somehow, H.S. Wing, a founding father of Kingfield and former owner of the Herbert Hotel, acquired the band stand. It was relocated close to a small, green embankment at the rear of his establishment where it remained "for approximately 80 years."

The band stand was purchased along with the hotel by Bud Dick. There it stayed until 1990 when Mr. Dick attempted to give the band stand to Kingfield's Recreation Board. The Board was a town agency and could not accept the gift on its own, so it was given directly to the town, though there was no land for it, no money to refurbish it, and no funds to maintain it.

Dan Davis, owner of One Stanley Avenue, then suggested the band stand be moved to his establishment, to be restored as a summerhouse for weddings and other special occasions. But the offer was not without controversy! Should the town give away a structure of historic value? Could funds be appropriated for the town to restore it? Finally, voters approved the sale to Davis by a vote of 136-4, with the stipulation that it never leave Kingfield. Not all voters were happy with this decision; an attempt was made to overturn the vote but to no avail.

On May 24, 1990 the Kingfield band stand was loaded onto a flatbed trailer and moved across the Carrabbassett River to One Stanley Avenue. The following spring, restoration was begun. New cedar shingles with copper edging as well as new latticework were part of the restoration.

The band stand is now—as it was in the beginning—in private hands.

Kingfield: The top photo shows two well-dressed young girls near the band stand, which has been electrified and has a fire hydrant handy: all the modern conveniences. Lawn swings adorn the yards, and signs advertise entertainment scheduled for July 28th. The band stand was later moved behind the popular Herbert Hotel (bottom photo).

An unidentified couple poses on the muddy roadway in front of the Kingfield band stand, perhaps recalling its early life at the local trotting park.

Lake View Plantation: and Milo

County: Piscataquis
Construction Date: c. 1900-1919
Builder: American Thread Company (?)
Original Location: Southern end of Schoodic Lake

LAKE VIEW PLANTATION—POPULATION 25—is traditionally the first town in Maine to record its vote for governor every four years. This remote area was organized in 1892 with 25,299 acres, but no road had yet been built, and the railroad line was not completed. The reason a village was carved out of this remote region was the need for a new source of fine birch trees to replace the supply at Egypt, Maine, fast being depleted by the Merrick Thread Company (later to become the American Thread Company). In 1892, Merrick produced 69,500,00 single spools!

By 1920, 52 homes, a hospital, general store, and fire department had been constructed and the population reached 200—the number necessary to be considered a township. The steam turbines of the mill generated the power used to operate the town's utilities and later, its streetlights. Lake View was an active factory village with a view of Mt. Katahdin. Strangely, there was no cemetery. What they did have was a community band stand!

The band

> was directed by Ralph Haskell whose four sons played in the group. On Saturday nights, concerts were held. The band was sometimes put on a barge or steamer and taken up the lake to play. At the plantation, the band had the use of a quaint band stand. The band sometimes ventured to outside points, like Camp Benson (near Newport). There they played with yet other bands, like that from Guilford.

- *Lake View Revisited* by William R. Sawtell

By 1902 the American Thread Company had exhausted the birch supply in the Lake View area. The company relocated, opening a new mill in Milo. This was devastating to the settlement of Lake View Plantation; in 1925 the entire town, including schools, municipal buildings, etc., were advertised for sale—all, that is, except the band stand!

Milo already had a band stand. It was of similar construction, and adjacent to Chase's Hall where many performing groups frequently came to entertain. In addition, another band stand had been built in 1908 at Milo Junction (Derby railroad station—cover photo). The band stand was likely just abandoned.

A newer gazebo is now located close to the original band stand site at Lake View's "Four Corners," from which the earlier structure disappeared.

Milo: This tall, two-story band stand was already in place when the American Thread Company relocated operations and residences here.

Lewiston: *A storm of protests*

County: Androscoggin
Construction Date: 1. c. 1870; 2. 1881
Builder: Unknown
Original Location: 1. City Park, moved to Lincoln Park
Current Location: 2. City Park, Pine and Park Streets
Description: 1. Hexagon (City/Lincoln Park); 2. Victorian

ONE OF MAINE'S MOST DECORATIVE BAND STANDS has fortunately survived at Lewiston. The Lewiston structure is described in *Maine Forms of Architecture*:

> In the parks of many cities and towns in the late 19th century, the band stand was a conspicuous ornament. Of the few surviving today the one in Lewiston City Park, dating from around 1881, is a splendid and well-maintained structure, proudly maintained and showcased for all to enjoy. Its cast-iron parts, decorated and painted dome, and polygonal shape lend a festive air to this "less than serious public monument."

Today the existing band stand still sports decorative pillars topping tapered brick columns. It remains as the single rare example of an early Maine band stand that was not constructed solely of wood. It is elaborately crafted with horseshoe trusses and ornate, fanciful, cast iron railings. Unfortunately, several pieces of the lavish, lyre-patterned ironwork that adorned the roof are missing. This distracts somewhat from its previous exotic look, when the band stand supported a bright red dome. This band stand is not the first located on this site; the first was apparently of a rarer hexagonal shape.

The date on the dome of the present band stand, 1861, is the year that the land for City Park was donated. It was gifted to the city by the Franklin Company, which used the great water power of Lewiston's falls to power its operations. According to maps of 1873, the green had been known as Flaggstaff Park. The name was changed to City Park and then to Kennedy Park after the assassination of President John Kennedy in 1963.

When the new band stand was erected at City Park in 1881, the older one was moved to Lincoln Park. The Lewiston Daily Sun reported on July 22, 1937 that

> ... without previous notice a crew of men under supervision of M. Dion started tearing down the bandstand on the Lincoln Street playgrounds at about 4 o'clock. A storm of protests resulted, but the razing process continued. Boards with nails in them are said to have been thrown about the playgrounds promiscuously and left there for the night.

The residents of that section of the city felt the band stand should have been preserved or "anyhow, we would like to know who gave the orders to have it torn down."

It would appear likely that composer Frederick G. Payne (1856–1919), organizer of the Lewiston Brigade Band and Payne's 2nd Regiment Band, played on both these band stands. He wrote more than 60 marches and waltzes and was the father of Hon. Frederick G. Payne Jr., Governor of Maine from 1949–1952.

Lewiston's first band stand at City Park was of the rare hexagon shape.

Lewiston: A stereo view of the original band stand at City Park as likely viewed from the upper floors of the old City Hall that burned and was replaced in 1890. The monument is known to have been erected in 1868 and this hexagon shaped band stand is also believed to be from the Civil War era. It was once moved about 30 feet and repainted.

Lewiston: The city was gifted with this ornate, band stand by the Franklin Company in 1881. This band stand and one located in the town of Andover (Page 51) are Maine's only remaining examples of Victorian-style band stands.

Limerick: *Traveling entertainment*

County: York
Construction Date: c. 1882
Builder: Unknown
Current Location: Intersection of Routes 5 near the intersection of Routes 11 and 160
Description: Gothic Revival

In May 1882 an editorial seeking town support for summer out-of-door concerts in Limerick ran in the Ossipee Valley News:

> There must be life enough in the village to raise the wherewithal to erect a band stand.

Life enough there was! Several photos exist of the many activities that took place in this band stand. Some—tumbling acts and tugs of war—seem out of character for such a charming structure! These photos are believed to have been taken around 1920, long after the band stand was first built, when townspeople were often entertained by traveling shows.

Although we cannot know precisely when Limerick's band stand was built, we know the 23-piece Limerick Cornet Band was organized in 1881. The band stand was likely built shortly after the above newspaper challenge was issued and was located near the "foot of the third Limerick Academy building."

Limerick: Traveling acts were very popular in the 1920s; tumbling and other acrobatics could even be performed in very small band stands, as this photo demonstrates.

One popular traveling attraction was Charles Hacker and Lester Gilpatric's internationally famous bicycle act. The duo also traveled with the Barnum and Bailey Circus.

The location, as well as the charm of the steeply sloped roof, is likely responsible for the many photos taken of the graceful, romantic-style structure. Today, builders of new gazebos call this an "English Garden" model. Its everted roof was not the most common form found in Maine, but it is the one we often visualize when band stands are mentioned and must have entailed extra work for local carpenters! Few examples have been found that use this roof slope; in addition to Limerick, one is preserved at Vinalhaven and similar styles were used at Milo, nearby Lake View, and Fryeburg.

Eventually, Limerick's band stand was moved back about 10 feet, lowered, and the stairs changed. Now, the town is debating its renovation: should the band stand be moved back to its original location? What color should it be painted? Everyone has an opinion.

Stories of boxing matches in the Limerick band stand are confirmed by this photo. The straw-hatted spectator appears to have enjoyed both performances—note his presence in the photo on page 116, too! (Photos courtesy Limerick Historical Society)

Millinocket: *Paper and peanuts*

County: Penobscot
Construction Date: c. 1923
Builder: Great Northern Paper Company
Current Location: Katahdin and Penobscot Avenues
Description: Neo-classical, well-maintained structure

MILLINOCKET WAS CHOSEN AS THE SITE OF A MILL, not a town. The band stand, as well as the earlier Great Northern Hotel, was built by Great Northern Paper Company as a showcase for the company's achievement in carving the town out of the wilderness. In 1889 contractors started to build the mill, and, by 1901, the town was incorporated.

The band stand was originally believed to have been built in 1928, but a recently discovered newspaper clipping reveals that this grand structure was actually built by the spring of 1923. It was described as "an octagonal granolithic structure that is of the most attractive in the state." It measures a grand $23\frac{1}{2}$ feet inside a perimeter of handsome cast iron railings. Great Northern engineers designed a neoclassic structure with Doric columns 20 inches in diameter at the base, which taper 12 feet upward. A cannonball-type finial tops the nearly flat roof. The fact that a paved parking lot now surrounds the band stand detracts from, but cannot destroy, the magnificent lines of this impressive band stand.

The location of the Millinocket band stand was previously a cemetery! Prior to construction of the park, graves were removed and the area was reconstructed as a town park with flowers, shade trees, and a brook that was dammed to make a pond. Before the band stand was built, children learned to swim at the wading pool and trains arrived nearby with circus horses and elephants.

James McLean recalls that his father came to Millinocket from Scotland and started work at Great Northern Paper Company in 1906. Decked out in kilts, he loved to sing Scottish songs, often performing in local minstrel shows.

McLean recalls that his father made a decision in 1916 that delighted everyone: he would order a peanut roaster! The excited family imagined selling hot roasted peanuts and making extra money, happily welcomed by everyone at the park.

The day that the raw peanuts arrived in their big 80 to100 pound bags was a big occasion! James couldn't wait. His father had designated him to be the "back tender" (a paper mill term). Days, and then weeks went by, the summer season passed, but the essential peanut roaster didn't come. Fearing they would go broke on this now uncertain project, the McLean family was forced to eat the unroasted peanuts!

The story had a happy ending. The roaster was finally delivered and pictures taken in 1920 show James, then $10\frac{1}{2}$, proudly working at his job as "back tender."

Later when the band stand was built, concerts became so popular that in 1947 the pond was filled in to make more seating room.

Millinocket: The grand band stand built by Great Northern Paper Company is the state's only surviving neoclassical band stand. Its fine detailing makes for an impressive structure.

Monson: *Early activities*

County: Piscataquis
Construction Date: c. 1930
Builder: Local labor
Current Location: Monson Academy; originally at Lake Hebron Hotel
Description: Two-story structure with slate roof

THE MONSON CORNET BAND was organized on September 15, 1887, and how they progressed! Band records show that the fourteen members of the band had become proficient so quickly that by the following summer they already had an active performing schedule in place. Highlights over the years included:

May 30, 1888	Memorial Day
June 18	Ladies gave a Benefit...raised $42
Aug 17	First out of town trip to play at Greenville Rally
Sept 1	County Mass at Dover, Hon. James G. Blaine, speaker.
Dec. 28	The G.A.R. Hall (where the band rehearsed) entirely destroyed by fire. A cornet, two drums and several music books lost.
May 13, 1889	First Uniforms purchased from Henderson & Co. Philadelphia. Navy blue trimmed with gilt braid.
May 15	First appearance in new uniforms
July 4	Band celebration, including music and drama at Tarr's Hall.
April 22, 1890	Concert, assisted by Miss Mammie Bush of Foxcroft, whistling soloist.
July 4, 1892	Furnished music for opening of Milo Driving Park.
June 28, 1893	Dedication of Soldier Monument at Abbott.
Oct. 21, 1903	Dedications of Soldiers Monument at Foxcroft
June 13, 1904	New set of uniforms purchased from Cincinnati Regalia Co. Dark blue trimmed with black mohair braid.
July 15	Band accompanied Onaway Lodge to Guilford for dedication of Odd Fellow's Hall
Sept 9, 1910	Band Concert at Penobscot Park
May 9, 1911	New set of uniforms. Regulation A.F. & M. uniforms and up to date in every particular.
Oct 1, 1912	Furnished music for the Centennial Parade.

The band's early success must have provoked some discussion among twelve young ladies of Monson who, as reported by *The Piscataquis Observer*, organized The Ladies Union Orchestra by December, 1888!

Monson's band stand was built around 1930, and appropriately, since the town was home to a slate factory, the new pavilion was roofed with slate, that has since kept the band stand in excellent condition. It was built on the lot owned by Fred Crane, on a site where the Lake Hebron Hotel once stood. George Pullen donated the lumber and townspeople donated time, labor, and other needed materials.

The music continued with band concerts every Thursday until June 21, 1944, when the band stand was moved in front of the Monson Academy building. The following summer saw Monson's most memorable celebration.

SURRENDER OF JAPAN CELEBRATED IN MONSON

Wednesday, August 15, was Monson's big day and the history of the town will record it as most outstanding. George Pullen, dressed as Uncle Sam, led the Monson Band, which ended with an effigy of Hirohito. The program for the afternoon was held at the band stand. Hundreds of cars parked upon the grounds and along the main street. The day ended with street dancing at seven o'clock in front of the band stand, this section having been roped off and traffic routed via Center Street and this lasted until late into the night. A highlight in the street dance was the presence of Mr. and Mrs. John R. Flint, octogenarians, who tripped the light fantastic along with the teenagers. The burning of Hirohito ended a great day around the Monson band stand.

— *Piscataquis Observer*, August 23, 1945

On June 21, 1988 the band stand was moved to its present location at the site of the old Monson Academy Building.

Monson: The band stand is still used, and money is being raised for its renovation.

Newfield: *The $100 band stand*

County: York
Construction Date: c. 1878
Builder: Citizen's Band
Current Location: Intersection of Route 11 and Elm Street
Description: Reproduction at Willowbrook at Newfield

FIRE DESTROYED NEWFIELD'S ORIGINAL BAND STAND. The reproduction that now stands at Willowbrook, the historic village, bears a sign that tells us how it originally came to be built.

> In April 1878, plans were made to solicit funds for building a bandstand through the efforts of the Citizens Band, an all-male brass band organized in 1876. When it was completed in May 1878 on a site near Route 11, the cost was close to $100. The band presented their first concert on Saturday evening, May 18, 1878.

> The Citizens Band was active until 1885. The later Cadet Band, in operation from about 1909–1914, was composed of both men and women. No bands were active in 1947 when the fire that destroyed most of Newfield also took the band stand.

Another band stand was known to be located at the Sandy Nook region near the corner of Acton Ridge Road and Libby Road. The mother of Earl H. (Steve) Day, a local man who developed the area, operated a farm with rooms to let. As part of the facility, a band stand was built on the grounds of the farm. It burned in the early 1900s.

Newfield: This reproduction band stand (above) is part of Willowbrook at Newfield, New England's largest restored 19th century museum village. At right is the original band stand shown before the 1947 fire.

Norridgewock: *A musical history*

County: Somerset
Construction Date: c. 1870
Builder: Unknown
Original Location: 1. Behind Firehouse Bakery;
2. Peets Corner, later moved across the street.

THE HANDWRITTEN TEXT OF A PAPER entitled "What Became of the Music?" is believed to have been written by Norridgewock historian Elizabeth Miller. She tells of early music in the town and her regret that family groups no longer made their own music singing around the piano, or young people around a campfire. She relates:

> In the early 1800s the south side of the river were blessed with the Hale and Hilton families, both having several talented musicians. Mr. Marshall Hale was a drummer in the Civil War and gained fame in several bands thereafter. Mr. Jonas Hilton was a fine violinist (as was Mr. Hale) and they frequently played for dances at the old Eaton School. They also organized a band which used to practice in the hall up over Hilton's shop on the corner of Main and Mechanic Streets. Directly across the Ooseola or Mill Stream, back of the present Firehouse Bakery, was a large willow tree of many branches. Here was built a band stand where the band gave concerts in the summer. Later a bandstand was erected at Peets Corner and then moved across to the corner above the Bank when the Civil War Monument was built. Various Norridgewock bands were featured there in concerts. The Norridgewock Band, Norridgewock Cadet Band, and Hobb's Military Band were some of the better known. After the Civil War and in the 1880s and 90s they were in much demand for GAR reunions, and band concerts all over the state. They made frequent appearances at Lakewood and the Pines on the Skowhegan Road (back of the present Sun Auto). In the late 1800s when the Coat Shops were flourishing, the lady workers made band uniforms and trimmed the shakos and caps for the Town Bands.

The second band stand is believed to have been moved by Charles Miller when the Village Improvement Society erected the War Monument to honor the Civil War dead. It sat for some time on the site now occupied by Norridgewock's World War II Honor Roll.

Norridgewock: Many band stands were topped with flagpoles.

Oakfield: *A volunteer effort*

County: Aroostook
Construction Date: 1911
Builder: Ezekial Benn and George White
Current Location: Next to the Universalist Church
Description: Second story added to open platform in 1915

THE STYLE OF SOME BAND STANDS just evolved to meet a need. The Oakfield band stand is a good example.

In 1910 the Bangor & Aroostook Railroad built a station at Oakfield that today is one of the company's three remaining wood frame railroad stations in Maine. The train that stopped at this junction on its way to Fort Kent brought visitors and settlers with it and was responsible for the town's expansion.

To better serve the expanding population, it was decided on May 29, 1911 to build a band stand on the lot adjacent to the new Universalist Church. The early construction was to be just one story, but not of an open style. The base had windows, most likely for selling baked goods, and the band played on the open top. William Shorey donated some lumber and the cement for the foundation, and Ezekial Benn and J. H. Holden furnished the rest of the lumber. Ezekial Benn and George White actually built it.

The band stand grew taller when Mr. White decided, in 1914–1915, to add a second story and a covering for the band stand. By 1916–17 the church had an active young people's Brass Band that had as many young women as men! Unfortunately, the band lasted only about ten years; however, the band stand was not moved or removed.

In keeping with the changing needs of Oakfield, the design was reconsidered in 1997. It was time for the town's centennial and the townspeople rallied once again. They wanted to renew the band stand that had been the center of their commuity so many years before. They also understood fully that the weight of today's bands and the need for electricity would not be well served by this restoration, but this did not deter them. They solved the issue by building a ground-level, open platform behind the old band stand to serve modern needs.

This time, it was Leroy Hersey who donated his labor and David and Foster Gordon who donated the lumber. Larry Greenlaw donated roofing supplies and paint. Once again, the band stand was built by a true community effort.

Today, Oakfield can boast proudly of restoring not only their charming band stand, but their historic Bangor & Aroostock Railroad depot, too.

1914-1915

1911

Oakfield: Part 1 was built in 1911, followed by a second story and roof in 1914-15. and finally in 1997 (not shown here) a platform suitable for contemporary bands.

Ocean Park/Old Orchard:
Religious revivals and the electric railway

County: York
Construction Date: 1898
Builder: Unknown
Original Location: 1. Ocean Park—Furber Park
2. Campground on 6th Street

AT THE TURN OF THE CENTURY, the church played an active part in the well-being of the body as well as the spirit. In 1873 a group of Methodists formed the Old Orchard Campground Association, and the Free Will Baptists established summer assemblies in 1881 at Ocean Park. This was part of the camp meeting movement that became well-known as "Chautauqua" after Chautauqua, New York's famous assembly. Nationwide, 350 assemblies existed, all located near water and amidst quiet, contemplative groves:

> A traveler, in search of quiet, leaves the brassy din and clatter of Old Orchard's continuous carnival and follows south along the white beach for a little over a mile. Turning inland at a right angle from the breakers he finds after a walk of five minutes from the shore a serene place among the pines with a rough-hewn tabernacle set in the midst and modest dwelling nearby.
>
> – *Story of Maine Baptists 1904-1954*, by Walter R. Cook

Transportation to Ocean Park was easily available. Trolleys served the village well between the days of horse and buggy and the auto era. The first horse-drawn trolleys started serving Old Orchard on July 4, 1888. From 1903-1938 the Biddeford and Saco Line picked up passengers every 15 minutes, making it possible for thousands to come to Ocean Park. It is known that these gatherings were highly promoted by the Boston and Maine Railroad; for example, an old B&M advertising piece promoted a "Christian Workers Conference at Ocean Park in July of 1908".

Furber Park, Ocean Park: Around the time that regular trolley service was established, the Ocean Park Improvement Society was founded to keep Temple Square clean and attractive. The Society also developed Furber Park, between Grand and Seaside Avenue, and built this steeply roofed band stand there. Young people gathered here on rainy days, and concerts featured the Salvation Army bands. An auxiliary fire hose on wheels made its shelter underneath. The band stand was removed in 1924 to make room for a library.

Furber Park, Curtis Home and Restaurant, Ocean Park, Old Orchard Beach, Me.

Old Orchard: Camp meetings often included concerts at an early Victorian band stand. Early views show it completely open, but by 1913 part of the band stand was glass-enclosed, perhaps to keep sheet music from blowing away! Postcards and daguerreotypes indicate that this band stand may have been one of the earliest structures on this property.

Old Town: *Public rest rooms?*

County: Penobscot
Construction Date: 1932
Builder: Citizens of Old Town
Current Location: Main Street/Old Town Riverfront Park
Description: 26' square; restrooms below

WHEN THE OLD TOWN BAND STAND WAS BUILT,

> it represented a significant community effort in 1932—a time of financial hardship and struggle resulting in civic pride and public projects such as the band stand.

The Old Town band stand's downward spiral and deterioration was a story typical of many Maine band stands. Because of its late construction date and the fact that it has recently been replaced with a reproduction, we know a lot about its structure. An Evaluations/Feasibility Study done by J. Gordon Architecture tells us that the tongue-and-groove decking of the floor sat on a 4 foot high wood-framed wall atop 4 foot high concrete foundation walls. This formed a basement with toilet facilities with entrances to the north for the ladies and to the south for gentlemen. This large, wood-framed, one-story structure—26 feet by 26 feet—had a post-and-beam frame, built entirely of softwood. It was of a square form with pyramid shaped roof. Benches were located inside horizontal railings, and stairs made the band stand accessible from both the east and west sides. Rafters were spaced from 16 inches near the corners to 28 inches at the center.

The band stand stood in a scenic setting near the Penobscot River and was the site of many concerts. Greg Osgood of the Bangor Band remembered fondly the concerts he played there, and not so fondly recalled that "the mosquitoes were big enough to carry off small game"!

By 1986, deterioration was evident. The lower level windows and entrances had been sealed off and the basement walls covered with clapboards. Railings for the steps were missing. Photos taken ten years later show more: the balustrades were gone, replaced with railings of an unmatched style; the interior benches appear to be gone, and shrubbery and landscaping were neglected. The old toilet facilities were long ago abandoned and the basement was full of debris and sand from river flooding.

Today, Old Town is completing a new band stand about 300 feet from its original site. The older band stand's former size, shape and integrity have been maintained, while meeting today's more stringent building codes. Plans to incorporate the old pyramid roof had to be abandoned due to difficulties in attaching it to the new structure.

When the old band stand came down, it was a surprise to many to learn that it had been used for other, more clandestine activities! With the trap door in the ceiling and a rope to shimmy up, young folks needed only to cut a hole in the roof for the smoke to go out. The old band stand had certainly found a more modern recreational use!

Old Town recently replaced this band stand with a well-planned reproduction.

Pittsfield: *The Hathorn Park March*

County: Somerset
Construction Date: c. 1920
Builder: GAR (?)
Current Location: Hathorn Park
Description: Extensively renovated

> Clyde Martin did a good job in proposing a public park on the old Hathorn Estate. It took nearly a year to sell the idea to the townspeople, but he kept at it and raised enough money to develop the first municipal park in Pittsfield.
>
> — *Pittsfield on the Sebasticook*

PITTSFIELD'S PARK LAND WAS ACQUIRED IN THE 1920s, and it is likely about this time that the band stand was built, or caused to be built by the Stephen Davis Post #11 of the GAR. Later, the park was dedicated to William Griffin, a school principal, band member and early leader of the Pittsfield Community Band. The park was memorialized by an early Pittsfield band member, who had studied under R. B. Hall: he wrote a march entitled "The Hathorn Park March."

At the request of the GAR veterans, the town later added granite steps leading into the park from Park Street. This was to allow the veterans to better care for the flag. The triangular concrete base that holds the new aluminum flagpole is the same footing that served as the base for the earlier wooden flagpole.

It is unknown whether the existing band stand incorporates any remnants of the original structure, since any written records are gone: fire has destroyed many of Pittsfield's town records. In more recent years, the band stand has seen only limited use, mostly as a reviewing stand for the Egg Festival parade, but the park itself hosts many other activities. A baseball diamond was added in 1950, a basketball court, playground, hotdog stand, and the Pittsfield Farmers' Market are added attractions. The band stand, now more commonly referred to as the "Gazebo," was renovated by Eagle Scouts during the early 1980s.

Pittsfield: The town "gazebo" as it looks today.

Portland: *Many fine band stands*

County: Cumberland
Construction Dates: See text
Builder: See below under individual parks
Current/Original Location: See below
Description: See below

SEVEN BAND STANDS are known to have been built in Portland during the Victorian era. They were built in the Queen Anne and Shingle styles popular at that time, and all had one feature in common: each was sited at a scenic location, either in a park or overlooking the harbor.

EASTERN PROMENADE (NORTHWEST END), FORT SUMNER PARK
This park, at the top of Munjoy Hill, was once the site of an early U.S. government seacoast fort. Efforts to turn it into park land began about 1880, and the band stand that was erected on this high point of land was one of the finest in Maine. It has been gone for many years.

EASTERN PROMENADE (NORTHEAST END), FORT ALLEN PARK
See page 60.

FORT MCKINLEY, c.1904-1990. Photo at right, below.

WESTERN PROMENADE
A different view of Portland Harbor was possible from the lookout on the City's Western Prom, on park land chosen for the Thomas B. Reed Monument, near Maine General Hospital. The band stand here was shingled, but heavier and lower to the ground than the one on the Eastern Prom. It was designed by John Calvin Stevens. See page 61.

GREENWOOD GARDENS, PEAKS ISLAND
Peaks Island had a beautiful park in the grove near where James W. Brackett took in summer boarders. Set among the trees was a small shingle-style band stand where Chandler's Band often played.

RIVERTON PARK
See page 76.

DEERING OAKS
See page 55.

Fort Sumner Park, Portland: The delicate, Queen Anne style band stand at Fort Sumner Park preceded the band stand built at nearby Fort Allen. (Photo courtesy Maine Historic Preservation Commission)

Fort McKinley, Great Diamond Island, Portland (Photo courtesy Kenneth Thompson, Jr.)

Round Pond/Bristol: *At the crossroads*

County: Lincoln
Construction Date: c. 1880s
Builder: Unknown
Original Location: Intersection of Routes 32 and Backshore Road, next to The Wright Stuff antique shop
Description: Vernacular

FOLKS AT ROUND POND found that, due to the influence of the wilder summer workers in the 1870s,

> Puritan ethics disappeared and locals began to spend more time in saloons and rumor has it there was a "cat house" at the Harbor View Motel.
>
> *– Thesis of Joshua Hanna, 1994*

Summer workers came because of the seven pogie and lobster canning factories and the granite quarries. Boarding houses all around the square housed quarry workers. This now-quiet town was on the stagecoach line from Damariscotta to Augusta, and there was a $1.00 round trip fare. Ruts from the stagecoach line can still be seen in the yard of the Harbor View Motel, now a bed and breakfast.

Some things have changed very little in Round Pond, one of seven villages in the town of Bristol. Granite Hall, built about a half mile from the granite quarries in the 1880s, was early on nicknamed "the saloon." This building remains much the same as it looked in the days when it was surrounded by other businesses, two hotels, the village green, and a band stand.

A visit upstairs at Granite Hall is a journey back to yesteryear. An old poster hanging on the wall declares that "The Great, Original New Orleans Minstrels Show" is coming to town. The stage is still in place, a reminder of days when traveling shows and silent movies provided great entertainment. Under owner William Fossett and later A.B. Smith, Granite Hall served as an ice cream parlor and barbershop, as well as a dance hall and even a roller skating rink.

Granite Hall fell on hard times after the quarries and the canning factories closed. The population diminished and there was little need for entertainment. In 1894, the versatile business was put up for sale: saloon, barber shop, pool and billiard tables, an organ, and much more—the price was $1,800. There were no immediate buyers, so the business continued to operate here at "The Square" in a much quieter manner.

Folks in Round Pond like Bethiah Callahan and Barbara Wilson remember walking by the town band stand on their way to get candy at Fossett's Ice Cream Parlor when they were young girls. And a delightful story tells of one Fourth of July in Round Pond when a group of young folks out "raising hell" picked up the band stand and "relocated" it in the field across the road!

Round Pond's band stand remained in the village on the path behind the Brown Church until the early 1940s. Its final demise is unsure; some stories have it torn down, but others tell of it ending up "down by the brook."

Round Pond: This band stand was likely built during the 1880s or 1890s, during the heyday of Round Pond. A new church steeple replaced the one that was blown off in 1869: visible in other photos, it helps to document the construction date. The band played oldtime tunes here on Sundays in the summer. Many early band members worked in the quarries; Perley Fossett played tuba.

Saco: *A four-season delight*

County: York
Construction Date: 1913
Builder: Unknown
Original Location: Pepperell Park
Description: Neoclassical

SACO CITIZENS SHOWED AN EARLY INTEREST IN MUSIC. While hymn books were scarce, it is stated that about 1730

> most congregations in Saco could sing five tunes—with greater or less harmony.

Saco also had a fine eye for architecture. The colonial revival style of the York National Bank (1896), the remodeled William Pike Block (1869), and the York Institute Museum (1926) reflect the work of noted architect John Calvin Stevens. It is no surprise then that the band stand built as the focal point of Pepperell Park was one of Maine's showiest; its roof was supported by twelve colonial style columns.

Historian Roy Fairfield remembers:

> As a boy growing up in Saco, I frequently attended Memorial Day and Fourth of July celebrations at Pepperell Park, and there I had my introduction to John Philip Sousa's music of which I became very fond—and still am. My mouth was always agape to watch the horn musicians, especially the tubas. I remember asking my dad how such human wind could make so loud and harmonic noises. My interest in Painchaud's band as a historical group derived from their playing at those celebrations. Such occasions when held in the evening were very festive because Japanese lanterns were strung all over the Park. I can still see the faces in the crowds of Saco citizens and their families gathered in the lawns facing the bandstand, the foci of the celebrations; also how brightly lighted they were during the fireworks ... also their spontaneous reactions, the oh's and ah's when the bombs "burst in midair," also the singing of the "Star Spangled Banner."
>
> Yet, in contrast: as a fourth and fifth grade student at Bonython and Jordan Schools, walking to and from my classes for two years, I can remember looking across the barren lawns winters when the snow-decorated bandstand looked like a wedding cake—a point of joyful memories in the bleakness of a never-ending snowy season.

Saco: The focal point of Pepperell Park was its classic band stand with unfluted columns, low railings, and a stairway for easy access.

Sherman Mills: *Stuck in the Mud*

County: Aroostook
Construction Date: c. 1909
Builder: Local labor
Current Location: Route 158, Sherman Mills
Description: Vernacular

IN 1984, SOME 75 YEARS AFTER IT WAS BUILT, the Sherman Mills band stand sat forlornly mired in mud—hardly an appropriate finish for a structure put up with so much community support.

Years ago, Irving Daggett drew up the original petition calling for the town to build a band stand, and Jeremiah O'Roak traveled on horseback from house to house to raise the necessary money. He collected $200 worth of small donations (25¢ to $1.00) and in 1909 volunteers built the once-proud band stand.

The town already had a park with elm trees planted on Arbor Day, May 10, 1895. The early band stand rose 8 feet to the band platform and then another 7 feet to the eaves. For seventy of its years it was the center of Sherman's Old Home Days.

Unfortunately the majestic elm trees succumbed to Dutch Elm Disease and had to be replaced with oak trees in May 1971. This was accomplished by the Molunkus Streams Fish and Game Club and the Molunkus Valley Federated Women's Club. But the band stand, the only historic structure left in Sherman Mills, continued to deteriorate.

In 1984, James Pratt, Lowell Smith, Roger Bouchard, James Leo King, James Ingalls, and Joseph Kelley, who knew of the early fund raising efforts one man had achieved, sat out to take up their own collection. The band stand would be restored!

With the first cash and supply donations, the men had the band stand pulled up out of the mud and set on a new cement foundation. Once the work was underway, donations started to flow in. New stairs were put on, the roof reshingled, the floor replaced and it was painted its original color, a deep forest green. In fact, the team collected more than the $1,200 they thought was needed and, in a move unheard of today, the excess donations were returned! In 1994 John Pocock reinforced the upper floor and support beams. These dedicated men continue to maintain their historic band stand.

At Old Home Days, townsfolk now work to serve hot dogs—sometimes up to 500 pounds—from inside their updated band stand. There is a remodeled kitchen with new pine walls and ceiling. Festivals are again accompanied by good old-fashioned music. Best of all, citizens can now resume neighborly efforts such as holding "cook sales" to help people burned out of their homes and carry on other fund-raising activities in the tried-and-true Maine manner.

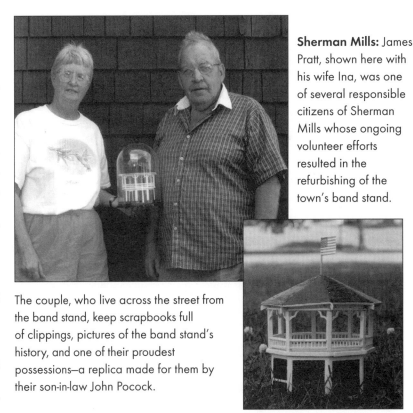

Sherman Mills: James Pratt, shown here with his wife Ina, was one of several responsible citizens of Sherman Mills whose ongoing volunteer efforts resulted in the refurbishing of the town's band stand.

The couple, who live across the street from the band stand, keep scrapbooks full of clippings, pictures of the band stand's history, and one of their proudest possessions—a replica made for them by their son-in-law John Pocock.

We Digress: Cannon Stories!

Sherman Mills: "OLD ZACH"

In the 1920s a target of Sherman pranksters was a pre-Civil War cannon called "Old Zach." It was named after the brilliant military leader, Zachary Taylor—later President (1849–50). The cannon is believed to have been given to the town around the time of the Aroostook War (1838-1840). It stood for eighty years in front of the post office.

Prior to Independence Day, pranksters would often hide the cannon and bring it out at midnight on the 4th to wake the whole town with its thunderous blasts and tremors. The noise was so deafening that some residents feared Sherman had been invaded by some foreign element. Dishes would break, windows shatter, and tempers flare.

Then came the year that the cannon mysteriously disappeared. Speculation as to its whereabouts circulated for fifty years. In 1975, The Bicentennial Committee of the Molunkus Valley Federated Women's Club was determined to find it in time to replace it for the town's 200th anniversary celebration. Older resident Theo Garnett, 80, chuckled to relate the story.

> **Prior to one July 4 we all traveled into town by the light of the moon to remove Old Zach from his station on the park. We transported him over the Gallison Road and hid him in the swamp located on the Beecher Sleeper farm where we planned for him to be safely hidden until a certain day.**
>
> **The boys in town also had definite plans for the particular date. They became aware of the cannon's disappearance. Acting upon intuition and rumors, they traversed to the Sleeper swamp with an improvised buckboard and released Old Zach from his murky surrounding and transported him back to town, where again he was placed in seclusion in the granary of the William Lewis General Store to await the celebration ...**

Still another group of boys

> **never allowed to go to the village "to carouse."... Upon hearing that the cannon was hidden in a camp near the old Gallison mill, they proceeded, without parental consent, to the spot not too far away from where the cannon reportedly was housed. Upon arriving at the campsite, they observed a padlocked door, flanked with two bobcat traps securely set, defying any predator to enter. ... They mustered up courage to peer through a window and there was Old Zach, sitting in all his glory, awaiting the next move ... The boys returned home without their parents being the wiser.**

– Newspaper clipping of June 17, 1975

It was never known which group was the last to have possession of this old relic, but with determination and a metal detector the cannon was found at last—forty-eight feet from the north end of the James Pratt home, buried $2\frac{1}{2}$ feet deep, just in time for the Bicentennial Celebration.

Today the cannon is proudly but firmly embedded in cement and set on the green near the band stand, but Old Zach no longer thunders through Sherman Mills on the Fourth of July!

Bath's cannon, shown in an old postcard view.

Dexter

Old cannons made powerful noisemakers for celebrating Independence Day. Many of these relics of the Revolutionary War were purchased and, after a few colorful escapades, were placed on village greens near town band stands. The *History of Damariscotta* relates that "these relics were scattered around the Boston Common and along the docks, and could be obtained at moderate cost."

A few verses from a poem written by Noah Burdick (1855-1911), who grew up in Dexter, would indicate that pranksters in that town also had a caper involving the town's cannon. Written in 1901, this poem probably refers to events from Burdick's life during the 1860s and 1870s.

The time they raised the big flag pole,
Up near the old town hall.
A monument of liberty,
The pride of great and small,

And when Old Glory they unfurled
On our great natal day
Ed Fifield trod all over my feet
A-hollering hooray.

That old brass cannon upon wheels,
That bellowed out its note
Upon the morn of July Fourth
From out its brazen throat,

One morn with pride they took it out
To make a mighty noise,
And wake within the breast of all
A glorious nation's joys.

They shot it hard, they shot it fast
With patriotism frought,
Not heeding that with constant fire
'Twas getting mighty hot.

Another shot was fatal now
And to that awestruck band
A premature discharge ensued
And took Hod Johnson's hand.

The boys one night that old gun stole
And took it to the hill,
They filled it up with stones and grass
As full as they could fill.

They pulled the string, an awful noise
That shook the very ground,
The cannon could not stand the strain,
In pieces it was found!

Corinth: Too Much Bang!

In East Corinth cannons were a dubious part of town celebrations. On July 5, 1932, the top story in the paper proclaimed "Three hurt, 1 critically when their cannon burst. Jack Brown, age 14, was standing near when loading the old cannon and is said to have been just ramming home a charge of powder, wadding it in with grass, when the explosion occurred."

South Portland: *Where are all the photos?*

County: Cumberland
Construction Date: 4 known locations and dates
Builder: Unknown
Original Location: see text
Description: See text

SEVEN NEIGHBORHOODS MADE UP SOUTH PORTLAND and several had their own band stands. One was at Ferry Village where the citizens supported Merriman's Band, formed in 1882 under the guidance of John Cole and Frank Collins. These men had an admirable reputation as fine musicians. Both were leaders of The Old Portland Band; Collins was also at one time leader of Chandler's Band and director of the band tournaments held at Lake Maranacook. Cole, a superior performer on the ophicleides, had been leader of the Fifth Cavalry Band under General Sheridan during the Civil War.

WILLARD SQUARE
As the fame of Merriman's Band grew, Edward Hays built them a second band stand at "Dog Corner," now known as Willard Square.

KNIGHTSVILLE
This neighborhood found new life with the erection of a small building with a large piazza close by the Knightsville end of the Portland Bridge. Charles Howe of Portland formed a band in 1885 and before long they were giving frequent concerts on that large piazza.

MILL CREEK
Much later, in 1944, South Portland acquired 8 acres at Knightsville as a memorial to the men and women who served in the Armed Services. It was filled in and named Mill Creek after a gristmill that once stood at the creek's mouth. The current band stand was built at this site around 1971.

Woodbury P. Harrington, left, who served as South Portland's City Clerk, was a professional musician for 40 years. Here he plays sousa horn with Harry Web, c. 1897. (Courtesy Maine Historical Society)

Turner: *Fun and games!*

County: Androscoggin
Construction Date: c. 1880
Builder: Unknown
Current Location: Intersection of Route 117 and "Old" Route 4
Description: See below

ONE COULD DRIVE RIGHT BY THIS SMALL INTERSECTION in North Turner and never suspect that from before the Civil War, for nearly three quarters of a century, it was home to the "old, old Band," the "old Band" and "the Band." We know from early records that there was also the North Turner Cadet Band, which had 23 men in 1880. At some point, it was provided with an unusual band stand—more a band "house." This building had windows all around and resembled a French gatekeeper's house. The instruments were stored here, and practice could take place within; however, for the most part, the band did its playing outside *(see page 28)*.

For many years, Turner was noted for its fine musicians, and its bands flourished. But in the 1920s, the bands had stopped playing. What was then to be done with the building? With the help of Maynard and Mrs. House, a social club was formed. Games and sports were a big part of community entertainment: checkers, croquet, cycling, canoeing, kite flying, and marbles were popular forms of enjoyment in that era, but in Turner, playing whist was really the rage! This card game, believed by some to be the forerunner of bridge, was wildly popular (a Bangor store is reported to have sold the amazing number of 4,600 Whist Pads!). Enough funds were raised that in the 1930s the band stand was cut in two and expanded so that the social club had a cozy place to play cards!

A photo taken about 1901 at a Lisbon Falls 4th of July shows the Turner Band in old-fashioned "cut-aways," gold-embroidered coat fronts, wide white belts, and ornate hats. Among their noted musicians was Ollie Wardwell, famous worldwide as John Philip Sousa's solo trombonist, and later a member of Arthur Pryor's Band of Philadelphia.

Turner: At North Turner, "near the old chair factory" and the GAR Hall is the old band stand. Today it is bypassed by Route 4.

Turner was also the birthplace, in 1818, of musician Luther Whiting Mason. While a young child, floods destroyed his family's forest land, and upon the death of Luther's father, the destitute family separated. Mason went to live with relatives in Gardiner, and grew up to become a self-taught musician. While teaching in Cincinnati, he was given a copy of C.H. Hohmann's *A Practical Course of Instruction in Music on School Principles*. This was the first graded course of music to be published in any language. From it Mason developed "The National Music Course," which would come to be used nationwide as a course of study.

In 1876 at the Philadelphia Centennial Exposition, Mason became interested in Japanese music and later traveled to Tokyo, where he became a national hero. A Japanese Consulate General testified as to Mason's importance:

> **The result of the Chinese-Japanese War (1894–1895) is due to Professor Mason's music. The Japanese troops sang "Hail Columbia," "America" and "Marching to Georgia" and won their battles.**

Professor Luther Mason, born in Turner, had taught them these songs.

Vinalhaven: *An island's remembrance*

County: Knox
Construction Date: 1895
Builder: W-14 Club
Current Location: Originally at corner of Main and Water Streets
Description: Queen Anne

EVERYTIME YOU TAKE A DRINK, THINGS LOOK DIFFERENT.

With this slogan on its parade wagon, we can only speculate what purpose united the W-14 Club: A men's drinking club? A temperance organization? The club's mission could have gone both ways! We do know that the club was formed the same year the W.C.T.U. and the Loyal Temperance Legion were organized on Vinalhaven. Whatever this organization's intent, we can be thankful for the band stand it erected in 1895.

Vinalhaven was flourishing after the Civil War, not only because of its fishing industry but also due to its nationally renowned granite quarries then in full operation. This island had a population of just over 1,600 and had sent 169 men to fight in the Civil War; 23 died for their country. Just as their mainland GAR counterparts, Vinalhaven men contributed greatly to the vitality and reconstruction of Maine. In 1870, the island built a granite monument honoring their lost brothers.

By 1870, Vinalhaven had organized a band, and the following Independence Day the group headed up the parade on a wagon drawn by 72 yoke of oxen!

In 1895 the GAR Memorial Hall was completed at a cost of $10,000. It housed a store and post office as well as a hall seating 600. It was dedicated on July 4th in an elaborate celebration that we can presume included a band concert at the newly constructed band stand on the corner of Main and Water Streets.

Since that time the band stand has continued to be used on Memorial Day and July 4th. Sometime before 1911, though, a move took place. The band stand was relocated up the hill onto the Village Common. It now looks across at the Civil War Monument and the Carnegie Granite Public Library, erected in 1906.

Vinalhaven: Since the summer of 1895, this band stand has been the site of summer concerts. Shown here at its original location, the band stand is flanked by the Reuben Carver Block (left) and the Moses Webster house (background).

Walter Cronkite at the Vinalhaven band stand for the town's 1989 Bicentennial Celebration. (Photos courtesy Vinalhaven Historical Society)

Vinalhaven: The residents of Vinalhaven still ponder the primary mission of the W-14 Club. Whatever their purpose, the Vinalhaven band stand was a prime accomplishment of these well-attired men (and their resident dog).

Yarmouth: *Builds another*

County: Cumberland
Construction Date: 3 known band stands
Builder: A.W. Longfellow
Original Location: See text; 3 known band stands
Description: See below

MONEY-RAISING EFFORTS TOOK PLACE IN YARMOUTH after the Civil War with the goal of erecting a suitable soldiers' monument near the Baptist Church triangle. General Joshua Chamberlain was invited to speak and gave his famous lecture on Gettysburg. It was not until after World War I that the statue was actually raised at the new site, opposite the Merrill Memorial Library.

It was also around this time that the band stand was erected.

This new band stand was Yarmouth's third. One early band stand is mentioned in *Old Times in North Yarmouth* as being at the town's train depot; the other was a Victorian band stand located at Riverside Cemetery *(see page ii)*. It is not known which of these was earlier, but it would be in keeping with the evolution of band stands in Maine that the first one was built at the resting place of Yarmouth's early war heroes.

On February 10, 1922, the office of A.W. Longfellow in Boston submitted a proposal for building Yarmouth's third band stand, and construction proceeded apace. It was dedicated on May 30, 1922. Plans were meticulous. The band stand was to be constructed of:

Cast Stone
- Columns, frieze, lower and upper members of brick base, setting for inscription table, treads, lower and upper risers of steps (2) to be cast stone with marble aggregate, sand finish.
- cast stone of base to go 6" below grade line shown

Slate
- Cover roof with No. 1 unfading green slate, 8" by $16\frac{1}{4}$" thick, drilled and fastened with two copper nails each, and laid not more than $6\frac{1}{2}$" to weather.
- All eaves and hips to be laid in elastic cement.
- Lay two courses of heavy roofing felt under all slates.

Copper & Metal Work
- Cornice, hip rolls, and finial to be of 18 oz. copper securely fastened.
- Provide and set plain wrought-iron rail where and as shown, securely fastened to the masonry.

Framing
- Framing to be of good spruce stock, free from loose knots, and spiked together in most secure manner.
- Pitch of roof to be accurately taken from drawing.
- Cover roof with first quality spruce boarding $\frac{7}{8}$" thick, matched and not too wide, planed on one side to an even thickness and well nailed breaking joints.

The dedicatory "green slate panel, set in cast stone" is now embedded in the wall at the VFW Hall in Yarmouth. It reads:

Memorial to Men of Yarmouth in War Service:
Revolutionary War 1775-1783, War of 1812, 1812-1814,
Civil War 1861-1865, Spanish War 1898-1898,
World War 1917-1919   erected A.D. 1922

Sadly, this band stand, one of the finest in the state, was allowed to deteriorate to the point of being a hazard. It had to be taken down.

Yarmouth's band stand, c.1922, bears a great similarity to one built in Millinocket, c.1923.

Band Stands: *In Revival*

During the 1920s, with the advent of the automobile and the popularity of new, indoor entertainment, many Americans saw the simple pleasures of small town entertainment as outdated. The world was opening wide. The growing sophistication of radio and soon television broadcasts spoke of the growing modernization of the country. Mass communication brought the world closer to home and, especially during the uncertain times of the two World Wars, the security of family grouped around the radio and television became more appealing than meeting neighbors at the band stand for a Saturday evening concert. Folks gathered inside, rather than out.

There were other reasons. The serenity of the outdoors was no longer friendly. Noises and exhaust fumes kept homeowners from enjoying fresh air out on the old front porch. "Inside" was air-conditioned and free of distraction—except, of course, for the television! For some, entertainment outside the house isn't necessary anymore, since cyberspace provides a virtual meeting hall, and video entertainment goes far beyond what our own village or town can provide.

Renewing and Rebuilding

Modern life is complex and exhausting as we rush from work to home, meeting multiple obligations. The idea of "close to home," "just good music" and a relaxing picnic on the lawn in the "good old summertime" sounds sadly ridiculous. Our modern mindset has contributed to the abandonment of those signposts of a slower age; as one consequence, band stands in many towns have fallen into disuse. As early as the 1980s few band stands were left throughout the state, and in fact there were fewer and fewer outdoor venues for musical performances. In the past decade, however, a longing for "the good from the past" has surfaced, which the events of September 11, 2001 have only accelerated. Front porches have started appearing on homes again. Neighbors and the idea of neighborhoods are being rediscovered. Happily, the idea of reviving a simple structure such as the humble band stand can be the start for a town to recover its sense of community, possibly even bring back the spirit of connection and good fun that has been gone too long from local neighborhoods.

And, in the good old American way, a band stand revival can even be seen as a fresh, new economic opportunity. Restaurants and shops are enthusiastic supporters of anything that encourages crowds of families and friends to gather in the center of town for wholesome entertainment. Enticing people away from TV and out of the house for some old-fashioned fun is good for business—a viewpoint not much different from the profit motive that had spurred railroads to build hotels and amusement areas at the turn of the century!

Let the next few pages be an inspiration. A new band stand, improved upon with modern construction and technology, can reconnect an unconnected town, generate new enthusiasm for local talent, bring after-hours business to small towns, introduce young ones to "uncanned" entertainment, showcase local artists, attract interest to an "undiscovered" town, and, in general, be an important part of reviving a town's spirit.

Not a bad result from such a modest structure!

Today, Still No Two Alike

Band stands newly constructed since the 1980s are as diverse as those built at the turn of the century. No two appear alike. In at least some cases, local carpenters with volunteer help, working without blueprints, are still responsible for design and construction.

Livermore: This large 32' band stand built in 1990 is topped with a lighthouse.

Fort Kent Riverside Park has a 17½' band stand built by the Lions Club.

Skowhegan: In 1900 this band stand was dedicated to the William Philbricks, Sr. and Jr.—longtime supporters of Coburn Park.

Brunswick: Built early in the band stand revival—1976—as a War Memorial.

Sullivan: Built in 1990 and topped with a sailing ship weathervane.

Cherryfield: Charles E. Wakefield Memorial Bandstand, 1994.

Richmond: A 1991 band stand overlooks the Kennebec River.

Building New

The idea may be old, but the price is new! Building codes, unheard of in the late 1800s and even into the early 1900s, now require many new considerations: structural capacity of roof framing, flood plain elevation, stairway riser and tread dimensions, baluster height and spacing, snow and wind loading requirements, and, of course, the Disabilities Act for Accessibility guidelines. The requirements make sense, but all require more than a modest expenditure.

Today there is also a pragmatic awareness that most outdoor band stands can present some serious structural and acoustical problems for musicians. Without a good design, visibility can be obstructed for both performing artists and their audiences. The classic bell-shaped roof structure can cause uneven audio levels and make it difficult to hear the total sound as a cohesive ensemble. A highly desirable sound setup sometimes uses diffuser panels, oriented to direct energy both outside of the band stand and back to the musicians. "The good the new brings with it" can also add considerably to the cost!

In 1999, Old Town undertook a Riverfront Project that included "doing something" with the old band stand. After a feasibility study that included the idea of renovating the structure, it was decided to build a reproduction band stand at an anticipated cost of about $47,000.

Bucksport originally considered a budget of $25,000 for a new band stand, but like so many public projects, money ran short. The actual cost was closer to $38,000—considerably more than in 1874, but less than some modern-day projects and a small price to pay for community togetherness!

North Yarmouth's band stand, built in 2001, was a joint effort of the town and the North Yarmouth Fire Department. With so many hours of volunteer labor contributed, the cost ran around $12,000. Several months later on a warm August evening, over 300 folks turned out for a concert. Babies in carriages, a toddler toting a toy guitar, seniors in lawn chairs, couples with blankets spread with picnic dinners, and groups of friends shared the moment while enjoying music provided by musicians Dan Merrill (who grew up in congenial North Yarmouth), Brian Johnson, and Barney Martin.

North Yarmouth: Dan Merrill and musical companions perform on the new band stand. While some might refer to it as a "gazebo," one North Yarmouth citizen commented, "our town is too small to have a gazebo. We just built an old-fashioned band stand."

There are other options for community entertainment. Some towns have chosen to build a "gazebo," a structure too small for a band and meant more as a picnic shelter. These are less expensive and can even be purchased ready-made. They may be complemented with a "band shell" made specifically to meet the needs for today's musical entertainment. Tents—which sheltered circuses and other traveling entertainment long before band stands came into vogue—are an attractive and versatile option and are available for rent on as "as needed" basis. Tents, however, are often meant for indoor rather than outdoor venues!

Towns continue to recreate band stands as community centers: some built on the town green, such as in Brunswick, Fairfield and Bath; and others—Lincolnville, Ellsworth, and Richmond—built at scenic waterfront locations not unlike those popular during the early 1920s.

Pranksters of today seldom hook on with a team of oxen and tow the old band stand away, but vandalism in the form of graffiti and structural damage can be a problem. A band stand endures best when it is in use all year round: when Boy Scouts use it to sell Christmas trees, garden clubs hold plant swaps in it, and town bands play in it during the summer. Oakfield holds a Strawberry Festival at the band stand, while in Millinocket, friends use theirs to gather for their Snowmobile Parade! The Easter Bunny and an egg hunt around the band stand can usher in spring, Frosty the Snowman is the sign that winter skating season has arrived, and at many towns children await Santa's arrival by fire engine at the lighted decorated band stand.

Band stands have that quality of endurance that makes them fit to survive and adapt to every generation. In July 1990, just before Russia's 1991 coup and the fall of Communism, 37 young boys and their music director from the Glinka Choir School braved the long journey to the United States from Leningrad. They arrived with not a cent of money, almost no English language skills, and, although arrangements had been made to meet them in New York, their flight touched down in Washington DC—three days ahead of schedule! Responding to the Choir's adversities, Bar Harbor citizens, along with the Arcady Music Festival, came together to help. It was a proud and enthusiastic crowd that welcomed the Leningrad Boys Choir at their first public appearance in the United States—on the band stand in Bar Harbor, Maine!

Today's band stands host assemblies with new concerns. It is the flag-draped place folks gathered to mourn the tragic losses at the World Trade Center in New York City and the appropriate place that thoughtful peace vigils took place as the threat of war with Iraq weighed heavily on many Maine minds. Once again, the town band stand is a fitting place to gather in commemoration, to debate, to express opinions, to celebrate or to mourn: part of a tradition that lasted for well over a century, and is now in the process of revival.

At band stands much like the ones where heroes of past wars were welcomed home, you can still hear the beat of patriotic marches. The town band plays again, its members joining together to keep alive a sound that starts toes tapping, faces smiling, and children running merrily round and round.

Today, vow that you will celebrate next summer with a concert on the village green. Bring a blanket, and maybe a picnic basket, chat with your neighbors, and sing along to "Alexander's Ragtime Band."

At the finale, when everyone stands for the "Star Spangled Banner," you'll understand the patriotic spirit that built Maine's first band stands.

Bar Harbor: The Leningrad Boys' Choir, for ages 10 to 13, was originally founded in 1479. In 1990, they were greeted in the Bar Harbor band stand in preparation for their first U.S. concert appearance.

The location of this photo, believed to be in Maine, remains unidentified. Some buildings in the background should help identify this picture. Is it your town? Where was it taken?.

BAND STANDS:
Gone, but not forgotten

We had one too!

I know it was there earlier than that!

That's not where it was.

THAT'S THE WAY NEW RESEARCH BEGINS.

It is with some misgivings that we publish this first band stand checklist, which we know to be incomplete. However, knowing it is only the first compilation, we anxiously await any information from the reader that will add to the inventory. Hopefully, it is a project without an end.

Small villages and towns throughout the state, as well as parks and other gathering spots in Maine's cities, may provide new stories. We look forward to receiving information about a community's proud heritage of life shared around a band stand. We anticipate more adventures of finding good photos of band stands whose stories are just now being brought to light and to locating the history surrounding band stand photos that still leave us in the dark.

Band Stands: A Checklist

A compilation of all band stands found to exist between 1874-1940, with approximate dates, and relevant information not previously covered.

Amherst: Photo dated July 4. 1921.

Amherst, Hancock County
Route 9, c. 1900-? East of town, across from the Town Hall, on town-owned land. Some remember a Grange Band that used to play there.

Andover, Oxford County
c.1890-present. (See page 51)

Ashland, Aroostook County
c.1937-present. (See page 91)

Athens, Franklin County
c.1904-present. (See page 92)

Auburn, Androscoggin County
Edward Little Park at Edward Little High School. c.1890-19?

Augusta, Kennebec County
c.1894. At Oakwoods Park, a very early trolley park established by the Augusta, Winthrop, and Gardiner Electric Line. This was at an area the old timers called "The Frog Pond."

Baileyville, Washington County
At Woodland Park, c.? In village of Woodland (not to be confused with the Woodland in Aroostook County).

Bangor, Penobscot County
1. Broadway Park, c.1890-?
2. Union Park, c. 1880-?
3. Chapin Park, c. 1898-?
(no photos of these first three parks)
4. Davenport Park c. 1900-?
5. Center Park, c.1881-?
Prominent Landscape Architect Frank M. Blaisdell was involved in the improvement of several of Bangor's parks.

Bar Harbor, Hancock County
c. 1899-present. (See page 97)

Bar Harbor: Photo prior to relocation.

Augusta: Oak Woods Park, an early trolley park.

Bath, Sagadahoc County
At Lincoln Park, intersection of Washington and Summer Streets. c.1883-1953?

Belfast, Waldo County
c.1890s-1930s. By City Pool, at Northport Avenue.

Bethel, Oxford County
Main and Mechanic Streets, c.1890-1907. The old band stand at Bethel Hill Village was taken down before the Civil War monument was erected in its place in 1908. This band stand was of special interest because it was said to have sported a canvas roof during the warmer months—almost a giant umbrella! (photo at Bethel Historical Society)

Biddeford, York County
Clifford Park, c.1915-early 1940s. On land purchased in 1894 from the Clifford family for $1,500.

Boothbay, Lincoln County
1. Bayville, a summer colony off Route 96 on Linnekin Bay, c. 1911-1950s?

Bayville (Boothbay): Photo dated August 23, 1939

Blue Hill, Hancock County
Intersection of Main and Union Streets, c.1884-1894. This very tall band stand was gone by 1895 when the town was developing this corner for the location of its Town Hall. (photo at Blue Hill Historical Society)

Bowdoin, Cumberland County
c. 1900s-? The Civil War Monument was dedicated in 1907. The celebration included a band that led the parade past the Bowdoin Center Store to the picnic grounds, located along the brook between the present day homes of Gerald and Laurance Adams. There was a band stand and a grove there that made it a very popular spot for public summer time affairs (*A Pictorial History of Bowdoin*). (no photo)

Bradley, Penobscot County
Intersection of Main and Bullen Streets, c. 1908-1928. Summer concerts were held nearly every week in the tall, roofed band stand, often by The Bradley Cornet Band. It was torn down in 1928 "due to disuse and disrepair." (obscured photo)

Brewer, Penobscot County
1. First Congregational Church and City Hall, c. 1900-?
2. Corner of Cove Street, c.1900 (present site of church parking lot). Recalled in a manuscript of the memoirs of eighth grade school teacher Dagney Erickson entitled *Happiness is Hindsight* is this information: "At the southeast corner, nearest the street, stood a tall band stand of later vintage, which in 1910 was sold to a chicken farmer who carted it away, then rebuilt into a dormitory for his hens." This band stand was likely gone before the bandstand at the paper mill site was built. (no photo)
3. South Main Street, South Brewer c.1915-? Close to the road in front of the Eastern Fine Paper Mill. Believed to have been built prior to WW1. (no photo)

Bridgton, Cumberland County
1. Intersection at top of Main Hill, 1863-?
2. High Street, 1877-1910. Moved to Post Office Square. (no good photos)

Bristol, Lincoln County
Round Pond, c. 1880s-late 1930s. At intersection of Route 32 and Backshore Road.

Brooksville, Hancock County
Route 176 across from Condon's Garage. c. 1890-1920s.

Brunswick, Cumberland County
North end of the Mall, c.1887-?. Before the word "mall" evoked images of retail stores and shopping, it had a quieter definition. A mall was a shaded place to walk, a fashionable promenade, and a place where pall-mall, a game similar to croquet, was played. Today in Brunswick you can see a mall, in its original glory, but this was not always the case. The area was once a bog—a disease ridden pond fenced off to keep cattle out. A "concert of frogs" was said to be the only music heard then. In the late 1880s, after diphtheria took its toll here, the area was filled in and a flagpole and fountain raised. At the north end, a band stand was erected, not far from the railway station, sometime before 1888. Today a large band stand built around 1976 overlooks the south end of the mall.

Calais, Washington County
c. 1900-present. Rebuilt. (see page 99)

Canton, Oxford County
Main Street, Route 108. c.? Photos show it during the floods of the 1920s or 1930s.

Cape Elizabeth, Cumberland County
1. Fort Williams, 1909-present. Restored in 1979 at a cost of approximately $25,000. (see page 100)
2. Fort Williams, 1911-?
3. Fort Williams, 1937-present. (see page 100)
4. Bowery Beach c.? Cresent Beach area. (no photo)
5. Cape Cottage Casino, Surf Rd., c.1898-? The casino, now a private home, was built by John Calvin Stevens and was frequented by soldiers from Fort Williams and trolley passengers looking for a fine shore dinner.

Caribou, Aroostook County
"The Square," intersection of Sweden, Main, and High Streets, c. 19?-1950s? The area is now a mall. Little is remembered of this structure. Some say it was moved to Teague Park during the urban renewal that took place around 1951, but others believe it has been gone since the late 1920s. Only Charles Hatch, age 92, could provide memories about going to concerts there with his mother and father when he was 6 or 7 years old.

Carmel, Penobscot County
Route 2 on right, 12 miles from Bangor, c. 1920s-late 1950s. Now the site of Doyan & Sons Auto and Truck Repair.

Casco, Cumberland County
Webbs Mills, Intersection of Routes 11 and 85, c. 1900-?

Castine, Hancock County
1. On the Common, c. ? An early open, square platform; history unknown. (obscured photo)
2. On grounds of the Acadian Hotel, Corner of Pleasant and Perkins Streets. c.1904?-1943. The large, ornate band stand in front of the "commodious" Acadian Hotel was convenient to the Steamboat Wharf and possibly was part of the expansion at the time when a second wing was added around 1904. The Hotel was formerly a house that was expanded to serve the growing number of summer guests. It was the site of many concerts until the hotel was torn down after a fire that occurred around 1943.

Caribou

Cherryfield, Washington County
1. Cherryfield Fairgrounds, c.1915-? Square, roofless (no photo).
2. Church Street, c.1938-1975. Near location of Union Trust Bank. Around 1956, the oldest band under the same name in the State of Maine (since 1869) ended its career and the band stand was given to the son of their first band leader, E.C. Wakefield. He in turn gave it to his son, a noted musician, Charles Wakefield, who recalls "... I placed an article in the Town Warrant asking if the Town would accept my equity in the band stand. This the Town voted to do, and was later forced into moving it to the back side of a town owned lot to make room for a Branch Office of the Union Trust Company. The band never did own the land where the band stand was located. Today (1975) the band stand is a lopsided wreck, slowly rotting, the only tangible evidence of one of the best known bands. Since the above date, the band stand has been demolished. It was my sad duty, a few years ago, to find a market for the instruments. They were sold to Paul Phelan, bandmaster of the Woodland Band. The proceeds were divided among those men who had played for twenty-five years or more. I still have the old valise that Father carried the music around in. It is intact and so is the old music." (from *Trademark: Music* by Charlie Wakefield). (no photo)

Corinna, Penobscot County
c. 1920-1955. Originally near Stewart Park, moved down to west end of Main Street across from Baxter Canning Company, now the location of the elementary school.

Corinth (East), Penobscot County
1. Intersection of Routes 11 and 15, c. 1870-1889. Location would have been near the terminal and repair barn for the trolley. Civil War veteran, Lyman Parkman, an itinerant bandleader founded a band there and gave them music lessons. He could have been responsible for building the band stand that was possibly destroyed in the fire of 1889. (no photo)
2. East Corinth Cemetery, c. 1900-present. (see page 49)

Cornish, York County
c. 1880-present. (no old photo) (see page 50)

Damariscotta, Lincoln County
Intersection of Business Route 1 and Bristol Road, c. 1900-1933.

Derby (See Milo)

Dexter, Penobscot County
1. Pleasantville Cemetery, c. 1895-?
2. In village, c. 1895-1940s? Corner of Zion's Hill and Main Street.

Dixfield, Oxford County
1. Dixfield, c. 1890-1940s. Weld Road near Route 2. (obscured photo at Historical Society)
2. East Dixfield, c. 1920s? Route 2, near Baptist Church.

Dover-Foxcroft, Piscataquis County
Foxcroft Academy Grounds, c. 1862-1904.

Dryden (see Wilton)

Durham, Androscoggin County
c.1888-present. (see page 105)

East Machias, Washington County
Hadley Lake Road and Main Street, c. 1930-? East Machias underwent a restoration during World War II. This included upgrading sidewalks from wood to concrete, the construction of a new library and much more. This was all during the time period when Roy Dennison, owner of the Arcade Theatre, was selectman. It is possible that this was when the band stand was built. Word has it that Donnie Small bought and resold it. (no photo)

Eastport, Washington County
c. 1890s-present. (see page iv.)

Exeter, Penobscot County
Near the intersection of Eaton Road and the Between-the-Mills Road, c. ?-1940s. Location was on the stage line from Bangor to Dexter and was the terminus of the stage line from Etna Station on the MCRR. It was an octagon-shaped band stand of the style that allowed for selling hotdogs from the first level. It was torn down in the 1940s. (no photo)

Fairfield, Somerset County
At Island Park, southern end of Bunkers Island, c. 1890-?

Falmouth, Cumberland County
Underwood Springs on the Foreside, c. ? This park had a "tea house" and possibly a band stand.

Farmington, Franklin County
1. c. 1874-present (see page 106).
2. Stanwood Park c. 1920s-1940s. Route 2, on knoll by Strawberry Fields Nursery.

Fort Fairfield, Aroostook County
Originally on Elm Street, c. 19?-1940s? Moved to Hunt Street to make room for the new post office. At the new location spectators could sit in the band stand to view the tennis games on three nearby courts. The overhead area was used for storage. (no photo)

Fort Kent, Aroostook County
c. ? (photos of the band stand during the flood of May 10, 1939 at Historical Society)

Foxcroft (see Dover-Foxcroft)

Fryeburg, Oxford County
At "The Pines," Bradley Park, c.1890?-1900. Featured a steeply pitched roof. (photo at Historical Society)

Gardiner, Kennebec County
On the Village Green, c. 1920s?-1950s. (photo at Maine Historic Preservation Commission, Augusta)

Harmony

Greenville, Piscataquis County
c. 1900-19? (photos at Moosehead Historical Society)

Hampden, Penobscot County
1. Riverside Park, Route 1A about $\frac{6}{10}$ mile beyond Avalon Village, c. 1898-1916.
2. Dorothea Dix Park, Route 1A. Liberty Pole erected July 5, 1899. A band stand built later on this site. (obscured photo)

Harmony, Somerset County
Post Office Square, Bailey Bridge Road, c. 1905-late 1940s. Harmony was at the very end of the Maine Central Railroad Line. It was appropriate that long-time railroad foreman "Gramps" Braley was Harmony's band director. There was little room at the intersection where the town band stand was located; horses, and later cars, parked right on the roadway. Traffic obviously was not a major concern; in fact, L. S. Cooley remembers: "Father bought a Model T in 1922, drove it for five years, sold it and went back to a horse and wagon for the rest of his life."

Harpswell, South, Sagadahoc County
At Route 123 opposite Hurricane Ridge Road, c.1920-?

Hartland, Somerset County
c.1900-present. Reconstructed band stand now on this site. (see page 36)

Houlton, Aroostook County
1. Market Square, c. 1895-?
2. Monument Park, c. 1905-19?

Island Falls, Aroostook County
Main Street near present site of Katahdin Bank, c.1900-1990s.

Jefferson, Lincoln County
c. 1910-present (see page 109)

Jemtland, Aroostook County
c. ? Possibly near the schoolhouse and home of Walter Hedman, leader of the New Sweden Band. (no photo)

Kennebunk, York County
In front of Unitarian Church, c.1870s-? This was an open platform, moved to the lawn of Mousam Tavern, Route 1. The band leader would only hire Republicans to work for him!

Kennebunkport Casino, York County
Unconfirmed.

Kezar Falls (see Parsonsfield)

Kingfield, Franklin County
c.1897-present. (see page 110)

Kittery, York County
Old Kittery Naval Ship Yard, in front of Barracks A and B. c.1900-?

Lakeview, Piscataquis County
End of Schoodic Lake, c.1900-19? (photo at Milo Historical Society)

Levant, Penobscot County
c.1900-? On August 14, 1913 "Walter Smith took great pains to see that the band stand was artistically draped and ornamented" for the centennial celebration. The town's early history includes The Levant Brass Band, which was playing in the last half of the 1800s, and in 1904 the Military Band Association Building is recorded as being sold to the Grange. (no photo)

Lewiston, Androscoggin County
1. City Park, c.1881-present. (see page 113)
2. Lincoln Park, c. 1870-1937. Moved from City Park to Liberty Street, possibly part of Railroad Park built in 1874.

Limerick, York County
c.1882-present. (see page 116)

Lincoln, Penobscot County
On Town Square next to Congregational Church, c. 1930s-1950s. Located in the yard of the primary school. It could be entered on the ground level and its platform accessed by interior stairs. It was likely built in the early 1930s and has been gone since the 1950s. (photo at Historical Society)

Lincolnville, Waldo County
c. 1890-? Open platform near present Honor Roll. The band dates to around 1870, and, because it was directed by singing teacher Dr. Benjamin Young, it became known as "The Singing Lincolnville Band." A "dance floor" was built in 1886 and was such a success that a building was put over it. Possibly this was the structure also referred to as the "band stand"? A large (36 foot) new band stand was dedicated in 2002 at Norton's Pond, Breezemore Park. John Silverio was the architect. Several present-day band members are direct descendents of the first band. (no photo)

Livermore, Androscoggin County
1. Livermore, at location of the present post office, Brettum Mills. c. 1900-?
2. Livermore Falls, corner of Main and Union Streets.

Locke Mills, Oxford County
On left near railroad tracks, c. 18-?-1919.

Lovell, Oxford County
Lower Main Street, Routes 93 and 5 triangle, c. 1900-1920s?

Lowell, Penobscot County
September 1937-? Built for the town's centennial. The Knights of Pythias Band played for the ceremony. (no photo)

Lubec, Washington County
c.1900-present. Current band stand is a reproduction built in the 1990s. (see page 52)

Lovell

Machias, Washington County
1. Near the jail on Court Steet, c.? Where a hotel was once located.
2. Near Route 192. intersection. (no photo)

Madison, Somerset County
Lakewood Theatre grounds, c. 1903-? In a wooded grove on Lake Wesserunsett. The band stand was at the end of the trolley line where Herbert Lindsay Swett, fresh out of Bowdoin, established an amusement center, menagerie, and bowling alley, as well as the theatre.

Madawaska Lake, Aroostook County
(P16, Range 4)
Shore Road between Stan's Store and the camps, c. 1894-1930s. Built by John J. Sodergren. In July 1894 Lewis Anderson wrote from Jemtland to Sweden that "I live at a lake where Peter and I have a steamboat to take people out on pleasure trips. They have Sunday School festivals, musical bands, a guitar band and a brass band and violins, singing and music and young people's groups every Friday evening and lovely prayer meetings." In 1895 the steamboat was sold, but others also operated steamboats, including Jacob Hedman and J.J. Sodergren, who also rented rowboats for the fabulous fishing. In 1899 J.J. was reported to be packing ice (from the lake, in sawdust in the icehouse) for the summer trade. He had also built a bandstand between the camps and the store, and provided transportation in his three-seater wagon for those without their own buggies (from Maine's Historic Swedish Colony website). John Sodergren's granddaughter Sylvia Carr remembers it from the 1930s as a roofless, wooden platform with waist-high railings and benches around the inside built by her grandfather. (no photo)

Milbridge, Washington County
Evergreen Cemetery, Route 1 south of town, c.1900-1960s. On Memorial Day, the procession would march out to the cemetery and would have music and a service for veterans. Later, it was located on Maine Street near the present site of the movie theater for a short while. It was moved to Bayside Park on Route 1A just before crossing the bridges. Charlie Wakefield's Band came to play occasionally, and the school band played there through the 1950s. It became a hangout for teens and fell into disrepair. By the 1960s it was gone. (no photo)

Millinocket, Penobscot County
c.1923-present. (see page 118)

Milo, Piscataquis County
1. High Street, East Milo, c. 1900-? Across from Historical Society.
2. Milo Junction (Derby), c. 1900-1940s. This area developed as a result of the Bangor and Aroostook situating its car shops there.

Monson, Piscataquis County
c.1930-present. (see page 119)

Naples, Cumberland County
On Route 302, on the village green, an earlier band stand preceded the present model. The old band stand has a new life on the water in Blair Watson's backyard.

Newfield, York County
1. Route 11 and Elm Streets, c. ? May 1878-1947.
2. Shady Lane: Acton Ridge Road and Libby Road, West Newfield.

Newport

New Gloucester, Cumberland County
1. Upper Gloucester, Routes 100 and 231, near Bald Hill Road, c.1900s-?
2. At Fairgrounds; questionable location. (no photos)

Newport, Penobscot County
Camp Benson, c. Aug. 1899-? Near Water and Bennett Streets. Builder: Grand Army of the Republic (GAR).

New Sweden, Aroostook County
Thomas Park, c. 1938-present. On Larson Road (old Route 161). Called the W.W. Thomas Band Shell. Walter Hedman was once leader of the New Sweden band.

Norridgewock, Somerset County
1. Behind Firehouse Bakery, c.? (no photo)
2. At Peets Corner. Moved across the street to site of present WWII Monument when Civil War monument was erected. c. ?

North Berwick, York County
Market and Main Streets (Route 9), c. pre-1916-?

Northport, Waldo County
Park Row, Bayside, c. 1920s? At playground on Penobscot Bay, This quaint village of gingerbread houses was a Methodist campground from 1849.

Oakfield, Aroostook County
c. May 1911-present. (see page 122)

Old Orchard Beach, York County
1. Ocean Park, Furber Park c.1894-1924. Present site of Library.
2. Salvation Army property, c. 1880s-? 6th Street, off Union Avenue.
3. Guild Park. A "pavilion" near present site of the war memorial covered bridge. Burned 1926. (no photo)

Old Town, Penobscot County
Main Street, Riverside Park (Binnette Park), c. 1932-1999.

Oxford, Oxford County
Intersection of High, Main, and King Streets, c. ?

Palermo, Waldo County
c. ? Unconfirmed.

Paris, Oxford County
1. Paris Hill. , c. 18?-? Roofless band stand, moved to Town Common in 1887 in front of First Baptist Church.
2. South Paris, on Market Square (formerly Central Square), c. 1880?-1906?

Parsonsfield (Kezar Falls), York County
At Garner Island in Great Ossipee River, c.1882-? Reached by a suspension walk running from the center of the covered bridge. (no photo)

Patten, Penobscot County
On Main Street, c. 1900-?

Pembroke, Washington County
1. West Pembroke, c. 1890s-?
2. Pembroke, c. 1894.-present. At "The Corner," now Front Street. Formerly located closer to the bridge, it has now been moved next to the American Legion Post #59. (no old photo)

Phillips, Franklin County
At intersection near the Church, c. 1890-?

Pittsfield, Somerset County
c. 1920-? Built or caused to be built by GAR Post. (no old photo) (see page 126)

Poland, Androscoggin County
At Poland Springs House (unconfirmed).

Portland, Cumberland County
1. Deering Oaks, c. 1883-1952. Northwest corner of the Park. Commissioned by William Goodwin.
2. Eastern Promenade, Fort Allen Park, c. 1890s-present. (see page 127)
3. Western Promenade, c. 1890-? Architect: John Calvin Stevens.
4. Fort Sumner Park, c.1900-? Top of Munjoy Hill.
5. Peaks Island, c.1880s-late 1930s? Greenwood Gardens, a grove belonging to James W. Brackett, who took in summer boarders.
6. Riverton Park, c.1896-? North of Portland on Presumpscot River. Landscape Artist: Frank M. Blaisdell
7. Fort McKinley, c. 1904-1990.

Presque Isle, Aroostook County
Near new courthouse and tracks of Bangor and Aroostook Railroad, c. ?-1957.

Rockport, Knox County
c. 1902-? Now Oakland Seashore Motel and Cottages, Dearborn Lane. Built by Rockland, Thomaston and Camden Street Railway.

Round Pond (see Bristol)

Saco, York County
At Pepperell Park, c. 1880s? Landscape Artist: Ernest W. Bowditch.

St. Albans, York County
Intersection of Main Street and Mason Corner Road, c.1900-late1920s?

Pembroke: Today

St. George, Lincoln County
At Long Cove, c. ? Long Cove is sometimes referred to as "Englishtown" because of the many Englishmen who worked at the granite quarries there. Later, Finns and Swedes became a prominent workforce. (no photo)

Sanford, York County
c.1937-present. (see page 23)

Searsport, Waldo County
Mosman Park, Water Street, c.1921-?

Sebec, Piscataquis County
At "end of lake," c.? (no photo)

Sherman, Aroostook County
c.1903-present. (see page 131)

Skowhegan, Somerset County
1. Coburn Park, c. 1920s-? Close to river.
2. Skowhegan Hotel, c. 1900-1950s. Elm Street, present site of Information Booth. Taken down c. 1954, and left on the lot where Wal-Mart now stands.

South Berwick, York County
At Quamphegan Park. c. 1900-?

South Portland, Cumberland County
1. Ferry Beach, c.?
2. Willard Beach, c.?
3. Knightsville, c.? (no photos of any)

Springvale, York County
Next to Butler Building on Bridge Street. c. 1890s-1901?

Stockholm, Aroostook County
1. By Lutheran Church, c. 1900
2. c. 1920-present. (see page 3)

Stockton Springs, Waldo County
At School Street intersection, c. 1900s-?

Togus, Kennebec County
1. Stick Style, c. 1875-?
2. Italianate Style, c. 1875-?
3. North Band Stand, c. 18-?
4. South Band Stand, c. 18-?

Turner, Androscoggin County
c. 1880-present. (see page 135)

Union, Knox County
.1894-present. (see page 50)

Van Buren, Aroostook County
c. ? The Silver Bell Band, organized in 1927, gave open concerts from Memorial Day to September and played for church affairs on both sides of the border. They built a large octagon band stand that was roofed and lighted, which cost the band $600 in addition to the free labor of its members. It was later moved to the American Legion lot and was used there for a few years for band concerts and a shelter for ice skaters until it was torn down by the Legion. Early photos, (likely 1920s) are said to show a band playing on the canopy over Clifford Gagnon's garage. The Silver Bell Band is said to have been the longest-lived Community Band on both side of the border—34 continuous years with the same director and manager, Anthony Ezzy (from *Van Buren History* by Martine A. Pelletier and Monica Dionne Ferretti). (no photo)

Vinalhaven, Knox County
1. c. 1895-present. (see page 136)
2. On Hurricane Island c.1910-? Described as "square, roofless."

Waldoboro, Knox County
"At the grove", c. June 1873-? There is also mention of a band stand erected in the village just east of the Sproul Block. The town is known to have built a band stand for the Centennial Celebration of June 26, 1873. The Cornet Band and the Goshen Band were engaged for the occasion. (no photo)

Waterville, Kennebec County
c. 1936-late 1940s? The R.B.Hall band shell was at the present site of the Alfond Boys and Girls Club. It was between the football field and swimming pool area. (no photo)

Washington Village, Knox County
c. August, 1911, "where the Central House had stood." Built for the Washington Centennial Celebration. (no photo)

Westbrook, Cumberland County
1. Warren Block, c. 18?–1882. At Main and Cumberland Streets (Cumberland Mills). Later photos show this band stand was replaced or a roof added at a later date.
2. Riverside Park, c. 1941. This late band stand provoked some 1970 memories by an unidentified observer: "East of the Legion Hall was a sunny, open field that looked as though it had been reserved for a ballfield. It had natural home run lines: in right, we used the Legion Hall grass line, always a bit longer than the manicured park lawn, and in left, the dirt path through the middle of the park. Few twelve year olds could reach Home Run distance consistently, but the thrill of power was within just power to slug a round-tripper. A significant disadvantage of this field was the prominent green and white bandstand positioned directly behind third base. Although the rafters of the bandstand served as an excellent gymnasium, a fact unfortunately never properly acknowledged by park administrators who have subsequently replaced it with an unremarkable structure of dubious esthethic value, the bandstand was an obstacle not unlike the Green Monster at Fenway. Shots down the line would ricochet back to the pitcher for an easy out, and fly balls that might otherwise be home runs would carom off its sloped roof. The present band stand was built in 1990.

Wilton, Franklin County
1. East Wilton, c.? Property now a playground, next to Fire Station.
2. Dryden, c.1887–? Adams Street and Route 15.

Winslow, Kennebec County
c. 19? At Tacconet Club, of Hollingsworth and Whitney Pulp and Paper Mill.

Winterport, Waldo County
c.19? (no photo)

Winthrop, Kennebec County
1. Marranacook, c. 19? At Spring House.
2. Island Park, c.1902–1940s.

Wiscasset, Lincoln County
c. 1900–? On Village Common, Route 1.

Woodland, Washington County (see Baileyville)

Yarmouth, Cumberland County
1. Railroad Depot, c.1880s? Grand Trunk line, Main Street. (no photo)
2. Riverside Cemetery, c. ? Route 88.
3. Memorial Green, c. 1922–195?
4. Prince's Point, 1920s. As remembered by Paul McIntire. Unconfirmed. (no photo)

York, York County
c.? (active in 1920s). Short Sands, at York Beach.

Fort Kent: Three men float by the band stand after the May 10, 1939 flood—one in white shirt and tie! (Photo courtesy Fort Kent Historical Society)

This book started as a compilation of photos from my private collection and information gathered on visits my husband and I made to almost every known or suspected band stand location in Maine—over 200 sites. We found libraries and historical societies filled with people who had never given band stands a second thought...never even known their town had a band stand! It wasn't long before "getting the mail" meant something other than bills and catalogs. Weekly, valued newspaper clippings, copies from scrapbooks, and personal notes arrived. Once alerted to the subject, peoples' eyes lit up with the idea of a new topic to research! The material I received has convinced me that there are still undiscovered band stands, and people who remember them. Sometimes memories conflict; sometimes even published accounts differ. Recording the history of Maine's historic band stands will not get easier with time, but with your help this material will evolve. Please contact me at stude28@downeast.net, or by writing to 12 Seely Road, Bar Harbor. Maine, 04609, telephone 207-288-3810.

Following my general references is a list of sources arranged by town. Because of the importance of every encounter and referral, no matter how brief, I have included here the names of many generous people and organizations who shared this journey with me. Some, who recounted memories over early morning coffee or in a casual encounter, never identified themselves; I wish that their names could be included here, too. I thank everyone: librarians, friends of friends of friends, even people of whom we asked travel directions. They all played a part in putting together this project. Let this nostalgic research continue to be improved upon.

General References

Automobile Legal Association. Automobile Green Book. Vol. 1, Boston, MA: Scarborough Motor Guide Company, 1920.

"Band Music from the Civil War Era". Retrieved July 7, 2001 from http://memory.loc.gov/ammen/cwmhtml

Cournoyer, Jill and Susan Gold. Make Way for the Automobile: The History of the Maine Automobile Association. Saco, ME: Custom Communications, 1998.

Clifford, Harold B. Maine and Her People. Freeport ME: Bond Wheelwright Co., 1958.

Dublin Seminar for New England Folklife Annual Proceedings 1996. "New England Music: The Public Sphere, 1600-1900". Boston University, edited by Peter Benes.

Edwards, George Thornton. Music and Musicians of Maine. Portland, ME: The Southworth Press, 1928.

Fleming, Ronald Lee and Lauri A. Halderman. On Common Ground. Cambridge, MA: The Harvard Common Press and The Townscape Institute, 1982.

Gilmore, Pascal Pearl. Memories of the Civil War. Private printing, 1928.

Hind, Harold C. The Brass Band. London: Hawkes, 1934, Revised edition 1952.

Kennebec Journal. "Maine and Her People". Historical Series II of VI, Lewiston, ME: July 3, 1976.

Lord, John Francis.ed. Revised Statutes of Maine. Portland, ME: 1848.

Maine Automobile Association. Maine Automobile Road Book and Pine Tree Tour. Portland, ME: 1914.

Maine Historical Society Collections. Portland, Maine

Maine Olmsted Alliance for Parks and Landscapes. Maine Survey of Historic Designed Landscapes, Phase I – Public Landscapes. Maine Historic Preservation Commission, 1993.

McAlester, Virginia and Lee. A Field Guide to American Houses. New York: Alfred A. Knopf, Inc. 1984.

Starr, Frederick S. ed. The Oberlin Book of Bandstands. Washington, DC: The Preservation Press, 1987.

Rutledge, Leigh W. "When My Grandmother Was a Child." n.d. newspaper clipping.

Shettleworth, Earle G. Jr. A Preliminary Historical Checklist of Landscape Architects in Maine. Supplement to Biographical Dictionary of Architects in Maine. 1987.

Smith, Diane. Positively Connecticut. Old Saybrook, CT: The Globe Pequot Press, 1998.

Sprague, John Francis. ed., pub. Sprague's Journal of Maine History. Dover, ME, 1922.

Wiggin, Hon. Edward. The History of Aroostook. Comp. by George H. Collins. Presque Isle, ME: Star and Howell Press, 1922.

"The Jack Daniel's Original Silver Cornet Band.". Retrieved January 31, 2003 from http// www.silvercornet.com/history.html

Varney, Geo.J. A Gazetteer of the State of Maine. Boston, MA: B.B. Russell Printing Co., 1881.

Warner, Maurice J. comp. Civil War Memorials Erected in the State of Maine. Maine Civil War Commission: 1965.

Wiggin, Frances Turgeon. Maine Composers and Their Music. Rockland, ME: The Bald Mountain Printing Co., 1959.

References and Acknowledgments by Town

Amherst- Amherst Historical Society, courtesy of Sylvia Sawyer.

Andover- Oxford County, Maine: A Guide to its Historic Architecture. Randall H. Bennett. Bethel, ME: 1984.

Ashland- History of Greater Ashland, Maine Area. Dena L. Winslow. York, ME: 1983. "Rededication of Ashland Community Bandstand to Charles Carter -July 9, 1987," Ashland Area Business Association.

Athens- A Historical Sketch of Athens, Maine Sesquicentennial 1804-1954.

Baileyville- Author's postcard collection.

Bangor- Woodsmen and Whig: Historic Images of Bangor. Abigail Ewing Zeltz and Marilyn Zoidis. Virginia Beach, VA: Donning Co.,1991. The City of Bangor, The Industries, Resources, Attractions and Business Life of Bangor and its Environs. Compiled and Pub. by Edward Mitchell. Newark, NJ: Blanding Industrial Journal Press, 1899. Bangor: Its Points of Interest and its Representative Business Men. George F. Bacon. Newark, NJ: Glenwood Publishers,1891. A Sketch of Bangor. George F. Godfrey. Boston, MA: James R. Osgood & Co., 1882. Images of America-The Twentieth Century. Vol. II. Richard R. Shaw. Dover, NH: Arcadia Publishing, 1997. Bangor Maine, 1769-1914: An Architectural History. Deborah Thompson. Univ. of Maine Press, 1988. Plan for Improvement of Broadway Park. Frank Blaisdell. 1898. The Journal of John Edwards Godfrey: 1870-1877. Vol. 11. Bangor, ME. Bangor Public Library, courtesy of Bill Cook. Personal communication re: recollections of musicians: Greg Osgood, Bob Jones, Woody Woodman, Bill Stetson and Bill Clark.

Bar Harbor- Discovering Old Bar Harbor and Acadia National Park. Ruth Ann Hill. Camden, ME: Down East Books, 1996. "The Band Stand," Bar Harbor Record. July 19, 1899. Bar Harbor Historical Society Collection, courtesy of Deborah Dyer.

Bath- The History of Bath. Henry W. Owen. Bath, ME: The Times Co., 1936. Maine Maritime Museum. Personal communication with Jane Whitten.

Belfast- Belfast Historical Society, courtesy of Andrew Keely.

Berwick- Old Berwick Historical Society, courtesy of Wendy Pirsig.

Bethel- Bethel Historical Society, courtesy of Randall Bennett.

Biddeford- Personal communication with Roy Fairfield.

Blue Hill- Blue Hill Historical Society Collection, courtesy of Nancy Stine.

Boothbay- History of Boothbay, and Boothbay Harbor, Maine. Francis B. Greene. Portland ME: Loring, Short & Harmon, 1906.

Bowdoin- A Pictorial History of Bowdoin, Maine:1788-1988 Bicentennial Book. Auburn, ME: Falcon Press, 1988.

Bradley-Bradley Maine Sesquicentennial 1835-1985. Bradley Historical Committee.

Brewer- Personal communication with Phyllis Scribner re: personal recollections of Eva Price and Leola Price Pearson.

Bridgton- Inserts from Scrapbook of Norman Libby, c. 1871-1911. Bridgton, Maine: 1768-1968. Bridgton Historical Society, Augusta, ME: KJ Printing, 1968.
Bristol- Personal communication with Sarah Herndon Scribner re: personal recollections of Bethiah Callahan and Barbara Wilson.
Brooksville- Personal communication with Thornton Gray and Isabel Condon.
Brunswick-The Old Photograph Series-Brunswick and Topsham. Joyce K Bibber. Pejepscot Historical Society, courtesy of Amy Poland.
Buckfield- A History of Buckfield. Alfred Cole and Charles F. Whitman. Lewiston, ME: The Journal Print Shop, 1915.
Calais- Personal communication re: recollections of Harry Lewis, Paul Phelan and Thelma Eye Brooks.
Canton- Personal communication with Everett Simpson.
Cape Elizabeth- Cape Elizabeth Past to Present. Compiled by Cape Elizabeth Historical Preservation Society. n.d. History of Cape Elizabeth, Maine. William B. Jordan Jr. Bowie, MD: Heritage Books Inc., 1987. Personal communication re: recollections of Lenora Bangert and Kenneth Thompson.
Caribou- Personal communication re: recollections of Charles Hatch, Lee Doody, Frederick Anderson.
Carmel- "Zoo-S-News," Carmel ME: Auto Rest Park Pub., July 4, 1937. "Stretch Your Legs," The Carmel Weekly. Jeff Shuls. March 5, 1994. Carmel Historical Society Collection, courtesy of Connie and Marvin Graves. Personal communication re: recollections of Carol McAlpine.
Casco - Author's postcard collection.
Castine- History of Castine. George A Wheeler M. D., Cornwall NY: private printing, 1923. History of Castine, Penobscot & Brooksville. George A Wheeler M. D. Revised edition, 1924. Castine Historical Society Collection.
Cherryfield- Cherryfield Soldiers Monument Exercises of Dedication: July 4, 1874. Portland ME: Bailey and Noyes Printing, c. 1875. Trademark: MUSIC. Charles E. Wakefield. Cherryfield ME: private printing, 1978. Milbridge Historical Society, courtesy of Terry Hussey and Dale Schevenieus.
Corinna- Personal communication with Lloyd Bolstridge and Everett Simpson.
Corinth- Personal communication re: recollections of Ena Chapman.
Cornish- More about Early Cornish. Compiled by Leola C. Ellis and Kera C. Millard.
Damariscotta- "The little cannon in Damariscotta," Lincoln County News. George F. Dow. Damariscotta Historical Society, courtesy of Richard B. Day. Personal communication with Donald and Charlene Hunter.
Dexter- Dexter Historical Society Museum Collection, courtesy of Rick Whitney and Carol Feurtado.
Dixfield- Personal communication re: recollections of Althea Fish and Aubrey Kilbreth. Dixfield Historical Society Collection.
Dover- Foxcroft- Personal communication with Celeste Hyer re: collection of M. Betts.
Durham- Personal communication with Maxine Herling. Untitled, Coastal Publishing Co. Inc. William Purrington. Oct 29, 1969. "History of Durham," Lewiston Journal Magazine Section. Dick Murray Oct. 23, 1965. History of Durham. Everett S. Stackpole. Lewiston Journal Co., 1899.
East Machias- Personal communication with Michael Hoyt and Earle Thomas.
Eastport- Personal collection of Ruth McInnis. Personal communication with John Grady.
Exeter- Personal communication re: recollections of Norman Buswell.
Fairfield- Fairfield Historical Society, courtesy of Richard Spear. Personal communication with Mark McPheeters.
Farmington- Personal communication with Ron Jahoda and Marjorie Goodwin.
Fort Fairfield- Pesonal communication with Scott Fields.
Fort Kent- Fort Kent Historical Society Collection, courtesy of Annette Daigle.
Fryeberg- Fryeburg Historical Society Collection, courtesy of Diane Jones.
Gardiner- Maine Preservation Commission Collection, courtesy of Earle Shettleworth, Jr.
Greenville- Greenville Historical Society, courtesy of Everett Parker.
Hampden- History of Riverside Park. Hampden, ME: 1898-1916. Richard Newcomb. Hampden, ME: Self published, 2001.
Harmony- Personal communication re: recollections of Elwood and L. S. Cooley.
Harpswell- Personal communication re: recollections of Althea Fish.
Hartland- Hartland, Maine, 1820-1970. Sesquicentennial Committee. 1970.
Houlton- The Story of Houlton. Cora M. Putnam. Portland ME: House of Falmouth, 1958. Maine Historical Society Collection. Personal communication with Frank Sleeper.
Island Falls- A History of Island Falls. Nina Sawyer. Private printing: 1972. Personal communication with Jean Grange Sawyer.
Jefferson- "Jefferson bandstand moved down mountain," The Lincoln County News. Pam Derringer. May 9, 1985. "Old Jefferson Bandstand Stirs Memories of Concerts Long Gone," Daily Kennebec Journal. Mrs. Paul Bond. August, July 19, 1967. "Jefferson Bandstand," Jefferson Town Report. Priscilla Bond and Martha Bond Tompkins. 1986. Jefferson Historical Society Collection.
Jempsted- Personal communication with John and Rosemary Hede.
Kennebunk- Brick Store Museum Collection.

Kingfield-Picture History of Kingfield: 1816-1980. Kingfield Photo History Book Association. "Funds ok'd for health agency," Sun-Journal. Jennifer Sullivan, May 22, 1990. "Historic gazebo finds new home," Irregular. Carol Engan. May 30, 1990. "Kingfield's battle of the bandstand", Morning Sentinel. Laura Dunham. Personal collection of Dan Davis.

Kittery- Images of America-Old Kittery. John D. Bardwell. Dover, NH: Arcadia Pub., 1995.

Lake View Plantation- A History of Lake View Maine and Lake View Revisited: A Centennial Book. William R Sawtell. Milo, ME: Milo Printing Co., 1985, 1991. Milo Historical Society Collection, courtesy of Gwen Bradeen.

Levant- Levant Maine: A History. Lynn Rogers and Patricia Pickard. Levant Historical Society, 1995.

Lewiston- The Peoples of Lewiston -Auburn 1875-1975. John A. Rand. Freeport ME: The Bond Wheelwright Co.,n.d. Historic Lewiston, Its Architectural Heritage. Ruth O'Halloran.The Lewiston Historical Committee, n.d. "Protest Tearing Down Lincoln St. Band Stand," Lewiston Daily Sun. July 22, 1937. Lewiston Public Library, courtesy of Lizette Leveille.

Limerick- "Limerick- Historical Notes" Linda Maule Taylor, ed. 1975. Limerick Historical Society Collection, courtesy of Del Floyd.

Lincoln- Lincoln Historical Society Collection, courtesy of Lawrence Sturgeon.

Lincolnville- Personal communication with Donald Heald .

Livermore-Livermore Public Library, courtesy of Penny Brown. Past Views of Livermore Maine. Livermore Bicentennial Comm., 1994.

Livermore Falls- Author's postcard collection.

Locke's Mills- Automobile Green Book. Vol. 1, Automobile Legal Association. Boston, MA: Scarborough Motor Guide Company, 1920.

Lovell- Personal communication with Roberta Chandler.

Lowell- Centennial Celebration Program.

Lubec- 200 years of Lubec History: 1776-1976. Ryerson and Lois Johnson. Lubec Historical Society, 1976. "Terror hits home," Bangor Daily News. September 13, 2002. Personal communication with Bernard Ross.

Machias- Personal communication with Michael Hoyt and Earle Thomas.

Madawaska Lake- Personal communication with Sylvia Carr, Rosemary and John Hede.

Madison- "The Early Days". Retrieved August 17, 2000 from www.skowhegan. org/skow/vacation/attractions/attractl7.html

Millinocket- Millinocket, Magic City of Maine's Wilderness. Dorothy Bowler Laverty. Freeport ME: The Bond Wheelwright Co., 1973. Personal communication re: recollections of James McLean. Millinocket Memorial Library, courtesy of John L. McManus.

Milbridge- Milbridge Historical Society, courtesy of Terry Hussey and Dale Schevenieus.

Milo- Milo Historical Society Collection, courtesy of Gwen Bradeen.

Monson- "Monson," Piscataquis Observer. Sept. 1884, and Jul. 4, 1889. "Ladies Orchestra Formed," Monson Newsletter. Spring 1999 reprint of December 27, 1888 edition of the Piscataquis Observer. Monson Academy Revisited:1847-1997. William R. Sawtell. Old Town ME: Howland's Printing, 1997. "Surrender of Japan Celebrated in Monson," Piscataquis Observer. August 23, 1945. Monson Historical Society Collection, courtesy of Estella Bennett.

Newfield- Personal communication with Elaine Hall. Willowbrook at Newfield.

New Gloucester- New Gloucester Historical Society Collection.

Newport- Personal communication with Gweneth Smith- Emery. Scrapbook of unidentified clippings. Newport Historical Society, Aug. 10, 1899.

New Sweden- Personal communication with John and Rosemary Hede. Personal communication with Niklas Roble re: conversation with Alwin Espling.

Norridgewock- "What Became of the Music?," unpublished paper credited to Elizabeth Miller. n.d. "Norridgewock Streets," unpublished paper: Norridgewock Historical Society Collection.

North Berwick- Personal communication with Curtis Goodwin and Bob Cole.

Northport- Author's postcard collection.

Oakfield- Oakfield Railroad Museum Collection, courtesy of Clyde Boutilier. Personal communication with Jean Grange Sawyer.

Old Orchard- "Plans of the Lands of Old Orchard Beach Camp Meeting Assoc.," Winfield Scott Dennett Civil Engineering. Saco ME: c. 1875. The Story of Maine Baptists 1904-1954. Walter R Cook. Waterville, ME: United Baptist Convention of Maine, 1954. All Aboard for Yesterday! A Nostalgic History of Railroading in Maine. Katrina H. Moore. Lewiston ME: Downeast Books, 1979. Story of Ocean Park. Adelbert Jakeman, Camden ME: Downeast Books, 1979. Centennial History of Old Orchard, Maine 1881-1981. Adelbert M. Jakeman. Ocean Park, ME: Ocean Park Association: 1981. "A Brief History of Ocean Park". Retrieved March 13, 2002 from http://www.oceanpark.org/history.html Personal communication with Steve Harding.

Old Town-"An Evaluation and Feasibility Study of: Old Town Band Stand," prepared for Save the Bandstand Committee. J. Gordon Architecture. Bangor, ME: 1999. Personal communication with Bill Osborne and Michael Graham.

Oxford- Personal communication with Margaret Ellsworth.

Paris- Pictorial History of Paris, Maine. Compiled by Paris Cape Historical Society. 1987. Portrait of Paris Hill. Martin Dibner. Paris Hill, ME: Paris Hill Press. 1990. Personal communication with Pat Chandler.

Parsonsfield- (Kezar Falls)- History of Porter. William Teg. Kezar Falls ME: Parsonsfield-Porter Historical Society, 1957. Personal communication with Pat Chandler and Ben Conant.
Patten- Personal communication with Jean Grange Sawyer and Carter Hall.
Pembroke- Historical Souvenir Book, Pembroke Sesquicentennial 1832-1982. Carl K. Hersey. Personal communication with Gail Menzel.
Phillips- Author's postcard collection.
Pittsfield- Pittsfield on the Sebasticook. Sanger M. Cook. Bangor ME: Furbush-Roberts Printing, 1966. Personal communication with Donald Hallenbeck.
Portland- "End of the Bandstand," Portland Evening Express. May 24, 1952. Scenic Gems of Maine. Portland ME: Geo W. Morris Pub., 1898. Bold Vision: The Development of the Parks of Portland Maine. Ed.H.Bill Holtwijk & Earle G. Shettleworth Jr. West Kennebunk ME: Phoenix Pub. 1999. Fifth Maine Regiment Center, Courtesy of Kim McIssac. Maine Preservation Commission, courtesy of Earle G. Shettleworth, Jr.
Presque Isle- Personal communication with Richard Graves.
Rockport- Personal communication with Barbara Dyer. "Oakland Park". Retrieved Jan. 23,2003 from http://www.rockland.villagesoup.com
Saco- Personal communication with Roy Fairfield and Tim Smith.
Saint Albans- History of St. Albans Maine 1799-1981. G. M Bigelow and R. M. Knowles. Brewer ME: Self published. L.H. Thompson Printers, 1982.
Saint George- "Long Cove, Penobscot Bay,Maine". Retrieved Feb. 9, 2003 from http://www.coastguides.com/r4/4.09LongCove.html
Sanford- Personal communication with Harland H. Eastman. Sanford and Springvale, Maine in the Days of Fred Philpot. Harland H. Eastman. 2nd ed. Sanford, ME: Wilson's Printers, 1993.
Searsport- Personal communication with Jane Whitten. Penobscot Marine Museum Collection.
Sebec- Old Sebec. William R. Sawtell. Old Town ME: Howlands Printing, 1999.
Sherman Mills- Personal collection of James and Ina Pratt.
Skowhegan- Personal communication with Maurice Valliere.
South Berwick- Personal communication with Charline Parsons.
South Paris (part of Paris)- Personal communication with Margaret Ellsworth.
South Portland- "Mill Creek Park," prepared by T.L Deman, J.d. Mitchell, and E. Richert, for the City of Portland. n.d. A History of Cape Elizabeth, Maine. William B. Jordan Jr. Portland ME: House of Falmouth Inc., 1965. Personal communication with Rosella Lovett.
Springvale- Personal communication with Harland H. Eastman. (See Sanford)
Stockholm-Personal communication with Frederick Anderson. Stockholm Museum collection, courtesy of Shirley Sjosedt.
Stockton Springs- Author's postcard collection.
Togus- Maine Preservation Commission Collection, courtesy of Earle Shettleworth Jr. Personal communication with Bedford Hayes.
Turner- Personal communication with Rufus Prince.
Union- 200 Years in Union. Chester Nash and Patricia Kahn. Rockland ME: Union Historical Society. 1974. "100th Anniversary Celebration: Band stand on Union Common 1895-1995," program. "Grange Refurbishes Historic Union Bandstand," Portland Sunday Telegram. Arley C. Clark. May 31, 1964. "Photo of Maine Band recalls Fourth of '90s," Portland Sunday Telegram. John Sherwood. May 31, 1964. Union Historical Society collection, courtesy of Suzy Shaub.
Van Buren- Van Buren History. Martine A. Pelletier and Monica Dionne Ferretti. Madawaska ME: St. John Valley Publishing Co. Inc., 1979.
Vinalhaven- Hurricane Island: The Town that Disappeared. Eleanor M. Richardson. Rockland ME: Island Institute, 1989. Vinalhaven Historical Society Collection, courtesy of Roy Heisler.
Waldoboro- Waldoborough, 1773-1973: 200 Anniversary: A Pictorial History. Esther Gross, ed. Waldoboro, ME: George Bliss Pub., 1973.
Washington Village- Welcome to Washington Village-Formerly Putnam, est. 1811. L. Murray Jamison. Washington, ME: Bicentennial Committee, 1976.
Waterville- Personal communication with Burns Hillman and Thelma Brooks Eye.
Westbrook- A Presence in the Community: The Warren Family Legacy. Anastasia S. Weigle. Westbrook ME: Warren Memorial Foundation and Cornelia Warren Community Assoc., 2000. Highlights of Westbrook History. Compiled by Ernest R. Rowe for Westbrook Womans Club. Portland, ME: Bowker Printing Co., 1952. Personal communication with Donna Conley, Julie Peterson and Phil Curran. "Westbrook Maine, the crew cut years". Retrieved November 22, 2002 from http://members.aol.com/sdhoy/TimePlaces/Westbrook.html
Wilton- Personal communication with Harold Karkos and Tony Nazar.
Winslow- Author's postcard collection.
Winthrop- 1771-1971 Winthrop History Book. Winthrop Bicentennial Committee. Lewiston ME: Kennebec Journal, 1971.
Wiscasset- Wiscasset in Pownalborough. Fannie Chase. Wiscasset, ME: The Southworth-Anthoensen Press, 1941.
Woodland- Author's postcard collection.
Yarmouth-Yarmouth Historical Society Collection, courtesy of Marilyn Hinckley. Ancient North Yarmouth and Yarmouth. William Hutchinson Rowe. Somersworth, NH: New England History Press, 1980.
York- Images of American Old York Beach, Vol.11. John D. Bardwell. Dover, NH: Arcadia Pub., 1995. "York County Extra," July 27, 2000.

Vinalhaven: Today, a new generation enjoys the old bandstand.

If a thing is old, it is a sign that it was fit to live, Old families, old customs, old styles, survive because they are fit to survive. The guarantee of continuity is quality. Submerge the good in a flood of the new and, the good will come back to join the good which the new brings with it. Old fashioned hospitality, old-fashioned politeness, old fashioned honor in business had qualities of survival. These will come back.

— *Capt. Edward V. Rickenbacker*

Index

NOTE: See also individual towns listed on pages 146-153, Band Stands: a Checklist.

A

AAA, 86
ALA, 85
Acadian Hotel, Castine, 58
Andover, 40, 41, 51
Ashland, 40, 90-91
Athens, 42, 85, 92-93
Augusta Cornet Band, 16
Auto Parks, modern, 87
Automobiles, effect of on band stands, 85-88
Automobile Association, Maine, 85

B

Band regalia, 18
    baldric, 18
    kepi, 18
    shako, 18
Band stand era, 29-48
Band stands
    architectural plans, example, Searsport, 34
    building process for, 43-44
    checklist of, 146-154
    definition of, 30
    different sizes of, 42-43
    history of, 1-10
    last hurrah, 85-88
    location of, 49-68
        celebrations, 64-66
        moving, 63-64
        parks, 53-58
        place of remembrance, 49-50
        town common, 50-53
    raising money for, 45-47
    revival of, 139-144
    building new, 142-143
    renewing and rebuilding, 139
    roofed, 35-40
    roofless, 30-34
    tourism and, 69-84
        grand hotels, 74
        railroads, 70-73
        steamships and summer colonies, 69
        trolley parks, 75-84
    types of, 30-41
Bangor, 65, 73, 85, 87, 94-95, 125, 135
    Broadway Park, 94
    Central Park, 95
    Chapin Park, 94
    Davenport Park, 94, 95
    Union Park, 94
Bangor Cadets (all female), 18
Bar Harbor, 42, 45, 96-97, 143
Bath, 98
Belfast, 57
"Blue Laws," 12
Biddeford, 56, 78
Bridgton, 5, 6-7, 18, 26, 31
    bands in, 7
Bristol Mills, 2
Brooksville, 68, 69
Brunswick, 141

C

Calais, 41, 99
Camp Benson, Newport, 41, 71
Canadian bands, 27
Cape Elizabeth, 100-101
Cape Rosier, Castine, 69
Casco, 65
Castine, 58, 69
Chandler's Band, 15
Cherryfield, 29, 47, 86, 141
Clifford Park, Biddeford, 56
Coburn Park, Skowhegan, 59
Corinna, 35
Corinth, 49
    cannons in, 133
Cornish, 50
Cumberland Mills, 4

D

Damariscotta, 69, 102-103, 133
Decoration Day/Memorial Day celebrations, 49
Deering Oaks, Portland, 55
Derby, 40, 48, 49, 63, 104, 112
Dexter, 25, 40, 43-44, 57
    cannons, 133
Dixfield, 57, 63, 104
Dover-Foxcroft, 31
Drum majors, 18
Dryden, 40, 50, 63, 70
Durham, 105

E

East Corinth, 49
Eastern Promenade, Portland, 60
Eastport, iv, 42, 99

F

Fairfield, 57, 81
Farmington, 88, 106
Fort Kent, 122, 140
Foxcroft, 31
    Foxcroft Academy Grounds, 31
Franklin Park, Portland, 53
Furber Park, Ocean Park, 123

G

Gardiner, 61
Goodall Park, Sanford, 23
Gowen Park, Sanford, 23
Grand Army of the Republic (GAR), ii, 8, 12, 43, 46, 49, 71
Grand hotels, 74
    Lake Maranacook Hotel, Winthrop, 74
Great Fire of 1866, Portland, 53
Greenville, 107

H

Hall, R.B., 66, 67
Hampden, 4, 79
Harpswell, 108
Hartland, 36, 64
Houlton, 8-9, 61
Hurricane Island, 25

I

Indian reservations, bands on, 27
International band stands, 30
    Mexico, "kiosco," 30
    Poland, "estrada," 30
International Order of Red Men, 46
Irish Band, 26
Island Falls, 63, 70, 73
Island Park, Winthrop, 25, 80
Island Pond, Fairfield, 81

J

Jefferson, 42, 109

K

Kingfield, 62, 110-111

L

Lake View Plantation/Milo, 112
Lakewood Summer Theater, 56
Lewiston, 26, 40, 41, 46, 113-115
    City Park, 113, 114
    Franklin Company, 115
Lewiston Brigade Band, 15
Liberty Poles, viii, 1-8, 31, 43
    Bridgton, 5
    Bristol Mills, 2
    Cumberland Mills, 4
    Stockholm, 3
    Stockton Springs, 4
Limerick, vi, 40, 116-117
Livermore, 140
Livermore Falls, 23, 42, 54
Locke(s) Mills, 84, 86
Lubec, 41, 46, 52

M

Machias, viii, 18
Millinocket, 23, 41, 42, 118, 138
Milo, cover
Modern Woodmen Band of Bridgton, 26
Monson, 119
Montcalm Band, 26
Mount Pleasant Cemetery, Dexter, 43, 48
Music in band stands, 11-28
    historical notes, 11-15
Musicmakers, ethnic, 25

N

National Home Band, 16; see also Togus Home Band
Native American bands, 27
Newfield, 45, 47, 120
Newport, 20, 41
Newport Band, 20
Norridgewock, 41, 63, 66, 121
North Berwick, 35
North Yarmouth, 142

O

Oakfield, 43, 122
Oakland Park, Rockport, 82-83
Ocean Park/Old Orchard, 123-124
Old Town, 27, 57, 125
Oxford, 32

P

Paris Hill, 63
Passamaquoddy Band, 27
Patten, 39, 63
Pavilions, 57
    Belfast, 57
    Dexter, 57
    Fairfield, 57
    Rockport, 57
    Skowhegan, 57
    York Beach, 57
Pembroke, 12, 38, 86
Phillips, 22
Pittsfield, 126
Pleasant Point (Eastport), 27
Poles and platforms, 4-9
Portland, 10, 53, 55, 61, 70, 74, 86, 90, 100, 127
    Deering Oaks, 127
    Eastern Promenade, Fort Allen Park, 127
    Eastern Promenade, Fort Sumner Park, 127
    Greenwood Gardens, Peaks Island, 127
    Riverton Park, 127
    Western Promenade, 61, 127
Portland Band, 12
Presque Isle, 21, 70, 72

Q

Quamphegan Amusement Park, South Berwick, 78

R

Railings, 41
Railroads, 70-73
    Bucksport, 70
    Camp Benson, Newport, 71
    Dryden, 70
    Presque Isle, 70

Richmond, 141
Riverside Cemetery, Yarmouth, ii
Riverside Park, Hampden, 79
Riverton Amusement Park, Portland, 88
Riverton Park, Portland, 76-77
Rockland Military Band, 21
Rockport, 57, 82-83
Roofed band stands, 35-39
    Corinna, 35
    Hartland, 36
    North Berwick, 35
    Patten Falls, 39
    Pembroke, 38
    South Paris, 37
Roofless band stands, 30-34
    Foxcroft, 31
    Oxford, 32
    Searsport, 33, 34
    Stockton Springs, 30, 33
    Winterport, 30
Roof styling, 40
    Carpenter Gothic, 40
    Colonial Revival, 40
    Gothic Revival, 40
    Italianate, 40
    Queen Anne, 40
    Stick style, 40
    Victorian, 40
Root, George F., 14
Round Pond, 60, 63, 69
Round Pond/Bristol, 128-129

S

Saco, 130, 141
Sanford Mills Band, 23
Sanford/Springvale, 23
Searsport, 30, 33, 34
Sebago Lake, 56
Sherman Mills, 40, 45, 131
    cannons, 132
Shingle style, 61
Silver Bell Band, 30
Sisters of Mercy, 27
Skowhegan, 56, 57, 59, 140
South Berwick, 78
South Brooksville, 68, 69
South Paris, 37
South Portland, 100, 134
    Knightsville, 134
    Mill Creek, 134
    Willard Square, 134
Springvale, 24
St. Albans, 64-66
St. Anne's Convent School, 27
Stanwood Park, Farmington, 88, back cover
Steamships and summer colonies, 69
    Cape Rosier, Castine, 69
Stevens, John Calvin, 4, 60, 61, 127, 130
Stockholm, 2, 3
Stockton Springs, 4, 30, 33
Sullivan, 141

T

30th Maine Fife and Drum Corps, 10
Togus, 16-17, 40
    North Band Stand, 17
    South Band Stand, 17
Togus Home Band, 16
Trolley parks, 75-84
    Augusta. 80
    Island Park, Winthrop, 80
    Island Pond, Fairfield, 81
    Oakland Park, Rockport, 82-83
    Riverside Park, Hampden, 79
    Riverton Park, Portland, 76-77
    York Beach, 75
Turner, 28, 135
Turner band, 28

U

Union, 19, 42, 50, 52
Union Cornet Band, 19

V

Victorian style, 51
Village Green, Gardiner, 61
Vinalhaven, 40, 117, 136-137, 160
Vinalhaven Band, 18

W

Webbs Mills (Casco), 65
Western Promenade, Portland, 61
Winterport, 30
Winthrop, 80
Wiscasset, 53
Women in bands, 18

Y

Yarmouth, ii, 15, 18, 50, 138
York Beach, 57, 75

About the Author

Barbara Fox has many musical memories. Her early life was spent in Canaan, Connecticut, and her musical family includes a father who played the banjo while rehearsing his act as "Mr. Bones" for local minstrel shows. Barbara spent summers with her maternal grandmother, an organist for Lutheran Sunday School in Raymertown, New York. These influences, along with several years of piano lessons, failed to reveal any talent of her own; however, Barbara is mother, grandmother, sister, stepmother, and mother-in-law to a lot of genuine musical talent!

Fox spent 32 years in the travel business, visited over 40 countries, and met many talented musicians. Several have visited her at her Bar Harbor home where, for 15 years, she served on the Board of Directors of the Arcady Music Society.

The daughter of a beloved first-grade school teacher and a banjo-strumming father who at 93 is "considering becoming a professional singer," Barbara is just the right person for the musical journey to uncover stories of Maine's band stands. And, even after retiring from the travel business, she can still stay within the state of Maine and visit Athens, Belfast, Naples, Paris…